W9-AQT-110

THE SMALL BUSINESS INCORPORATION KIT

Also Available by Robert L. Davidson, III

The Small Business Bankruptcy Kit
The Small Business Partnership Kit
Contracting Your Services
How to Start Your Own S Corporation

THE SMALL BUSINESS INCORPORATION KIT

Robert L. Davidson III

John Wiley & Sons, Inc.

New York • Chichester • Brisbane • Toronto • Singapore

In recognition of the importance of preserving what has been written, it is a policy of John Wiley & Sons, Inc., to have books of enduring value published in the United States printed on acid-free paper, and we exert our best efforts to that end.

This publication is designed to provide accurate and authoritative information in regard to the subject matter covered. It is sold with the understanding that the publisher is not engaged in rendering legal, accounting, or other professional services. If legal advice or other expert assistance is required, the services of a competent professional person should be sought. *From a Declaration of Principles jointly adopted by a Committee of the American Bar Association and a Committee of Publishers.*

Library of Congress Cataloging-in-Publication Data

Davidson, Robert L., III.
The small business incorporation kit / by Robert L. Davidson, III.
p. cm.
Includes index.
ISBN 0-471-57651-4 (alk. paper). — ISBN 0-471-57652-2 (pbk. : alk. paper)
1. Incorporation—United States—Popular works. 2. Corporation law—United States—Popular works. I. Title.
KF1420.Z9D38 1992
346.73'06622—dc20
[347.3066622] 92-14054

Printed in the United States of America

10 9 8 7 6 5 4 3 2 1

Preface

Congratulations! The fact that you are reading this book is evidence of your desire to control your own fate, to start and run a business in which you play a major role. The corporation, the subject of this book, is a popular form for the small business and offers a number of advantages, such as the corporate shield to protect you from major business liabilities and the "S" type corporation where profits flow directly through to the shareholders.

By the time you finish reading this book, you will know more about what a corporation is than do most business people. You will know how to form your own corporation, how to prepare the articles of incorporation and bylaws, what your freedoms and your constraints are, and more. And you will have insight into the role of your silent partner, the IRS, in the operation of your business.

Where the waters of commerce are murky, namely for the legal niceties and for the tricks of the trade in tax planning, this book will help you select and communicate with professionals, such as lawyers, tax advisors, and CPAs.

Good luck.

ROBERT L. DAVIDSON, III

ABOUT THE AUTHOR

Robert L. Davidson, III, is an attorney and publications consultant in Princeton, New Jersey, where he specializes in author–publisher contracts, small business law, and elder law.

He is author, coauthor, editor, or coeditor of 13 books, the most recent of which are *Contracting Your Services, The Small Business Partnership Kit, The Small Business Bankruptcy Kit,* and (coauthored with Arnold S. Goldstein) *How to Start Your Own S Corporation*, all published by John Wiley & Sons.

Mr. Davidson holds degrees of Bachelor and Master of Science in Chemical Engineering from the University of Missouri, and a Juris Doctor degree from Fordham University School of Law. He is licensed to practice law in New Jersey, is a member of the American Bar Association and the New Jersey State Bar Association, and of Tau Beta Pi (engineering), Sigma Xi (science), and Alpha Chi Sigma (chemistry) honor societies.

CONTENTS

THE SMALL BUSINESS INCORPORATION KIT

SECTION I

INTRODUCTION TO CORPORATIONS

CHAPTER 1

WHAT "INCORPORATION" MEANS

WHAT IS A CORPORATION?

A corporation is an *artificial person* with a legal life of its own, separate from the role or life of any living person. For that reason, a corporation is said to be immortal, unless your *Articles of Incorporation* say otherwise. A corporation continues to survive the loss of an owner (*shareholder*) through retirement, death, or sellout.

In contrast to other business forms, such as a *partnership* or a *sole proprietorship* (both discussed later), the corporation is a formal legal creation, whereas the other forms have laws that must be followed once formed, but no formal statutory procedures of formation. The partnership is covered in detail in *The Small Business Partnership Kit*, by Robert L. Davidson, III (John Wiley & Sons, 1992).

Corporations are formed according to state laws, each state having its own special requirements, and you can incorporate in one state only. To conduct your business in another state, you will have to meet that other state's requirements for filing as a *foreign* (out-of-state) corporation. There is no federal law of incorporation, although once incorporated, there is the federal tax code and other laws that must be observed.

The powers allowable to a corporation for the conduct and management of its business are much the same as for a natural person, as long as they are consistent with the Articles of Incorporation and the laws of the state in which incorporated. Included are the powers to:

- Sue, be sued, and defend against suits and complaints.
- Make, adopt, and amend bylaws.
- Deal with real or personal property and property interests.
- Deal with shares or interests of other entities.
- Enter into contracts and guarantees, and incur liabilities.
- Lend and invest money.

- Pay pensions, and establish compensation and benefit plans.
- Make charitable donations.

There are other powers, of course. The list in total will vary according to the statutes of the state in which you are incorporated.

TYPES OF CORPORATION

Several types of corporations are of immediate interest to the small businessperson considering incorporation. They include:

- Public (or "C") Corporation.
- "S" (or Subchapter S) Corporation.
- Professional Service Corporation.
- Closely Held Corporation.
- Personal Holding Corporation.

There are also special incorporation laws for nonprofit and not-for-profit corporations, as well as those representing financial institutions, insurance companies, municipalities, and more. These, however, are beyond the scope of the small business and will not be covered in this book.

THE CORPORATE SHIELD

The major advantage most often cited for incorporation is the *limited liability* afforded by the *corporate shield* (also known as the *corporate veil*), which, short of criminal activity or personal misfeasance, protects the personal assets of the shareholder owners from the debts or insolvency of the corporation. Creditors to the corporation are not permitted to collect corporation debts by suing individual shareholders of the corporation.

Piercing the Corporate Shield

Don't be fooled, however, into believing that the corporate shield is otherwise complete protection. If you had an unincorporated business with debts and then converted your business into a corporation, you will continue to be personally liable for the debts of your former unincorporated business, even after incorporation. Also, if you are starting up a new small business, some lenders will require that you provide a personal guarantee based on your personal assets before they will lend to your new enterprise.

The corporate shield will not protect an officer or director from unpermitted or illegal acts in the name of the corporation. The Internal Revenue Code (IRC) levies penalties against officers and other "responsible persons" who fail to withhold and pay employment taxes due the federal government. And should the board of directors declare an "illegal" dividend, creditors and preferred shareholders adversely affected may sue the directors, either singly or as a group.

Personal illegalities, such as price fixing or other crimes, are not protected by the corporate shield. Even shareholders themselves may be liable for debts if it appears that the corporation was organized and operated with insufficient capital to meet reasonably anticipated obligations. When a shareholder or a small group of shareholders (such as in a closely held corporation) operate the corporation as a "personal alter ego" by commingling funds, or fail to follow procedures according to the Articles of Incorporation or by-laws, the IRS may try to penetrate the corporate shield and tax the shareholders as individuals.

The answer? Simple. Be honest; don't commit any crimes in the name of the corporation. Keep your personal affairs and your corporation affairs, particularly your banking affairs, separate. See that your withholding taxes are paid promptly. Play fair with all classes of shareholders.

When would limited liability afforded by the corporate shield be most helpful for you? It can be valuable if your business is engaged in some high-risk activity that, because of its nature, can create personal or property damage and lawsuits; or if you cannot find an insurer to cover you; or if you cannot afford the insurance premiums.

EASE OF OWNERSHIP TRANSFER

Another advantage is the ease with which ownership can be transferred upon the retirement or death of a shareholder. The continued life of the corporation does not suffer or end, as in the cases of partnerships and sole proprietorships.

DISADVANTAGES OF INCORPORATION

The major disadvantage most often cited against incorporation is *double taxation*, namely the fact that corporate profits are taxed before being distributed as dividends to shareholders, then taxed again as income to the shareholders. Another disadvantage is the added bookkeeping and tax-reporting complexity of a corporation, as contrasted with a partnership or sole proprietorship. As a corporation, you will be inundated by a blizzard of federal, state, and local tax forms and withholding reports, even if you have no profit.

A seldom heard potential problem with incorporation arises with insolvency and the filing of a bankruptcy petition. In a Chapter 7 (termination and liquidation of the business) bankruptcy or a Chapter 11 (reorganization of the business) bankruptcy, the corporation is barred from many of the debt-discharge (cancellation) advantages that can be found in Chapter 12 (family-farmer payment plan) bankruptcy or Chapter 13 (wage-earner payment plan) bankruptcy.

OTHER CORPORATE FORMS

The C (or Public) Corporation is the most commonly met form. But if you are starting with a small business that will not be immediately profitable, you may wish to elect to convert your C corporation into an S corporation where profits and losses flow directly to you, much as in a partnership, without the double taxation. See *How to Start*

Your Own S Corporation by Arnold S. Goldstein and Robert L. Davidson, III (John Wiley & Sons, 1992) for details on S corporations.

If you are a licensed professional, such as a doctor, dentist, lawyer, or architect, you may wish to form a professional service corporation where all the owners belong to the same profession.

OTHER FORMS OF BUSINESS

There are other forms for your business, such as the *partnership* and the *sole proprietorship*. Before you settle definitely on incorporation, you should also consider them. The sole proprietorship is the most common and the simplest business form. Next in popularity is the partnership.

What Is a Partnership?

A partnership is a business that is owned by two or more persons who, as co-owners, carry on a trade or business for profit.

There has been very little change in the laws governing partnerships since the U.S. Congress enacted the Partnership Act in 1890. The most modern version, the Uniform Partnership Act (UPA) was approved in 1914 by the National Conference of Commissioners of Uniform State Laws. Most of the 50 states, the District of Columbia, and several U.S. territories have adopted some version of the UPA. In 1916, the Uniform Limited Partnership Act was approved, and versions of it too have been adopted by most of the 50 states, the District of Columbia, and several U.S. territories.

The General Partnership Although normally just called a partnership, the word "general" shows that it is not a limited partnership. It is not incorporated and thus has none of the protection of a corporation, but also very few of the disadvantages of a corporation. Each full (or general) partner has the legal right to perform all acts needed to operate the partnership business, unless otherwise agreed.

There is no law that requires you to ask official permission to form a partnership, nor do you have to file your partnership agreement with any federal, state, or local governmental agency. Don't be fooled, however, in thinking that there are no legal requirements or controls. The details and concepts of partnerships are discussed in detail, along with guidance in drafting a partnership agreement, in *The Small Business Partnership Kit* by Robert L. Davidson, III (John Wiley & Sons, 1992).

The primary advantages of a partnership are its simplicity when compared with a corporation, and its use of multiple skills when compared with a sole proprietorship. You will have fewer governmental forms to cope with than for a corporation, and your profits will be drained by the double taxation faced by a corporation. Unlike a corporation, a partnership does not have to register as a *foreign* (out-of-state) operation to do business in a state other than the one where it is formed.

Partners share profits or losses in proportion to their ownership of the partnership. While the partnership must file an annual tax return, the partnership itself does not pay taxes. Profits and losses pass through to the individual partners to be reported on their personal tax returns. This is particularly attractive during the early stages of the partnership when your share of the partnership losses can be applied against your income from other sources.

There is a potential disadvantage with a partnership, namely the threat of unlimited liability for debts or other claims against the partnership should it become insolvent or involved in expensive legal claims. If the partnership business lacks the money needed to pay a creditor, that creditor can lay claim to your personal assets, and those of your partners, to satisfy the debt. Or, if in conducting partnership business, property is damaged or some person is injured by you or by a partner or by someone employed by your partnership, the partners will be liable.

If all the partners are available and have sufficient personal funds, the debt or court judgment payment will be in relation to the individual percentage ownerships in the partnership. But what if you are the only one with money or property? Or what if the other partners disappear? The total amount of the claim can be made against you alone. This is called *joint and several liability.*

If one of your partners leaves the partnership for any reason, either voluntarily or involuntarily, or you add a partner, by law the partnership is automatically dissolved. This does not mean that the business of the partnership must cease, however, if provisions are included in the partnership agreement for continuing the business.

The Limited Partnership Limited partnerships are formed by full partners to raise money from investors. Limited partners buy shares of the profits or losses of the partnership, limited to (calculated by) the amounts they invest.

The limited partners have no voice in the management of the partnership, but if there are losses, unpaid debts, or court judgments, their liabilities are no greater than the amounts they have invested. Their personal assets cannot be attacked and attached.

The Sole Proprietorship

Sole means only or alone. A sole proprietorship is a business owned solely by one person. You, as owner, can hire and fire employees. You may delegate the management of the business to an employee, and you may share profits with employees.

As owner of a sole proprietorship, you are boss. You are the sole decision maker. Success or failure lies on your shoulders alone. You alone are liable for all debts, taxes, and other business liabilities. If one of your employees harms a person or property in connection with his or her duties with your business, you are the one who will be held legally liable.

As is true for the partnership, the sole proprietorship does not pay taxes. All profits and losses from the business pass through to you, the owner, to be reported on your personal income tax return. If you have income from other sources, you can apply losses from the business against this income.

If you, the owner die, the sole proprietorship ends. For this reason, it is important that you make provisions in your will or otherwise to either sell the assets or transfer them to someone. If your business assets are left by a will, and your heirs want to continue the business, delays in probating your will may harm the business.

MAKING THE DECISION

Before you decide for or against the corporation form for your business, here are some important questions you should ask yourself:

- Do you need to work with others, or can you do it by yourself? If you need to add other skills or resources to yours, where will you find them? How will you attract them?
- Is there a risk to the business? What is it? What does it mean to you financially? Can you bear the risk?
- Is it important to you to maintain control? Or are you willing to share control with others?
- How will you finance the business? Can you find backing by yourself? Or will you need money or facilities held by others? Will banks or other lenders support you by yourself? Or will you need co-owners to back you?

Finally, but most important, how well do you know yourself? Would you be happiest with a sole proprietorship where you have total control, but also total responsibility? How are you at working with others as equals if your business idea needs skills that add to and blend with yours? Are you a plunger by nature, or are you supercautious?

CHAPTER 2

GETTING STARTED

THE IMPORTANCE OF GOOD ADVICE

Should you hire an attorney to help you incorporate, or can you do it yourself? Should you pay for an accountant to help you set up your business-and tax-record bookkeeping system, or do it yourself? The answers to these questions will depend on your personal experience and training, the interrelationships of the incorporators and shareholders, and the complexity of your business operation.

When to Use a Personal Lawyer

Does a business need the advice and services of a lawyer? Possibly not, if your business has limited legal and financial liabilities. If your corporation business will be cutting grass or washing windows, you won't be involved in complicated contracts and leases. And you do not need a lawyer to purchase liability insurance to cover any physical or property damage your activities might cause.

But if you are involved in leasing facilities and equipment, if you are stocking inventories and working materials, if you are signing high-dollar-amount construction or service contracts, if you are dealing in employee contracts, if you will be dealing with union labor, you need the advice and assistance of a lawyer.

You will face a dozen or more legal technicalities as you plan and operate your corporation. Some you will recognize, others you will not. Some situations that appear simple to you may be fraught with legal complexities, and you will never know until it is too late. An innocent failure to observe a single statute or regulation can cause immense trouble. The simple failure to obtain a certificate of occupancy for the purposes of your business may lead to a fine or penalty, or could close down your operations temporarily, even permanently.

Start to use your personal lawyer with your articles of incorporation agreement. Your attorney can help you select a legally acceptable name for your corporation and can aid you in the drafting of your articles of incorporation to match your present business objectives, yet not limit future growth. Your attorney will assist you in developing your corporation bylaws (rules of operation), and should you decide to seek financing by a public offer, your attorney will see that you do not violate applicable laws. Before you file your incorporation papers, you will be well advised to consult with a lawyer who has experience not only in corporation law, but with the type and size of your proposed business.

Continue consulting your lawyer with the operation of your business. You will be signing leases for facilities and equipment. You will be purchasing supplies and furnishings. You will be making deals with customers for your product or service, you will be negotiating and signing sales or service agreements. All these activities entail contracts, and contract law is a world unto itself. If the stakes are too high for you to risk loss, see your lawyer. If there is possible future liability not visible to you at negotiation time, your lawyer can forewarn and advise you. And more.

When to Use a Personal Tax Advisor

If your corporation is a simple operation working out of your basement or garage, you may feel that a tax advisor, such as a CPA (Certified Public Accountant) is a luxury. Perhaps so, perhaps not. A good tax advisor is worth his or her weight in gold, and not only can guide you past tax-record danger spots but can help you plan legal tax-saving strategies relating to income, expenditures, and more.

If you will have employees or will be hiring and paying independent contractors, your business and tax record keeping can become quite complex, considering withholding taxes, unemployment taxes, social security taxes, worker's compensation insurance, medical and pension benefits, state and federal tax returns, and more. You will need professional help to set up your system and to modify it with time as your business grows and changes. Your tax advisor can help you prepare your business plan and can show you how to best present the capabilities and potentialities of your business when approaching banks for credit lines or loans.

How to Select Your Advisors

There are several simple common-sense rules when selecting your legal and accounting advisors:

1. Find persons you can get along with.
2. Find persons who show an interest in you and your needs.
3. Find persons with experience in the needs of corporations.
4. Find persons with experience in your type of business.
5. Find persons who will be available when you need them.
6. Find persons you can afford.

Once you have located these individuals, be sure that you have a complete understanding of how you will work with them. What will they do for you? What will they charge you? When should you contact them? What will you be expected to do in return? What will you do when they are ill or otherwise unavailable?

"TERMS OF ART" GLOSSARY

The legal meanings of words and phrases often contain concepts and subtle innuendos that are not immediately obvious from the general dictionary definitions of these words. The following terms, important to the understanding of incorporation law, are defined according to their usages for creating corporations. The words in italic type within definitions are defined elsewhere in this listing.

accrual method financial recordkeeping system that credits income when earned or due and expenses when incurred, regardless of actual cash receipts or disbursements (see also *cash method*)

active income income received as the result of ongoing active efforts (see also *passive income/loss*)

adjusted basis original cost adjusted by additions and depreciation (see also *basis*)

advance notice notice of an intended action given in advance of the actual action (see also *constructive notice* and *notice*)

agency a relation in which one person (or organization) acts for or represents another by the other's authority; a relationship of principal and agent, or master and servant

alternative minimum tax taxation rule assuring that a certain minimum tax will be paid, regardless of tax credits and other tax preferences

appreciation unearned increase in the value of property due to inflation or other market factors (see also *goodwill*)

arbitration method for settling a dispute by a quasi-judicial procedure as provided by law or agreement; arbitrator's judgment usually binding on all parties (see also *mediation*)

articles of incorporation document by which a private corporation is formed under state incorporation laws

asset in business and commerce, everything that can be made available for the payment of debts

assumed business name name for a business other than the name or names of the owners of the business

balance sheet financial statement to show the true state of a particular business

basis in general terms, the initial cost or purchase price (see also *adjusted basis*)

board of directors in a corporation, an official body with the duty and authority to set policies, appoint corporate officers; generally responsible for the actions of the officers

bond certificate or other evidence of debt; a *debt security*

book value the value of company assets after deducting all liabilities

breach of agreement see *breach of contract*

breach of contract failure without legal excuse to perform a promise contained in a valid contract, either written or oral

Bulk Sales Act statute designed to prevent the secret sale in bulk of a business's goods or inventory to defraud creditors

business name trade name or commercial name used to identify a specific business

bylaws regulations, ordinances, rules, or laws adopted to govern an association or corporation

C corporation used to differentiate between a regular incorporation and the election to be an *S corporation*; also known as public corporation

capital [assets] actual property or monies invested or undivided assets for the operation of a business

capital gain sale of a capital asset in excess of appraisal value or costs

cash method [bookkeeping] financial record-keeping system relying on actual cash receipts or actual cash disbursements at the time of receipt or disbursement (see also *accrual method*)

certificate of incorporation term used with or in place of *articles of incorporation*

closely held corporation small corporation with a limited number shareholders and having no general market for selling shares in the corporation

commingling of funds placing of funds for several purposes (such as personal with business, or trust with personal) in a single fund or account

common stock stock in a corporation where the stock does not have a dividend preference, as for *preferred stock*

consideration reason or material cause (e.g., payment of money) for entering into a contract (e.g., a sale or other transaction)

constructive notice openly available facts or events from which a reasonably alert and aware person should have notice of the existence of a situation (see also *notice*)

contract labor persons or organizations who are not employees of the hiring business who have contracted to perform specified duties for the hiring business

conveyance of interest transfer of rights or property free of conditions

copyright right of literary property as recognized by law; categorized as *intellectual property*

corporate shield protection of personal assets from business liabilities through incorporation

corporate veil see *corporate shield*

corporation "artificial person" created under the authority of law; normally an association of a number of persons (the *shareholders*) and surviving the resignation or death of any one of the shareholders (see also *C corporation, S corporation*)

cumulative voting system of voting, as for members of the corporation board of directors, in which a person voting has a number of votes equal to the number of directors to be chosen and is allowed to concentrate the entire number of such votes upon one candidate

DBA abbreviation for *doing-business-as*

debt security document or other proof for the loan of money to an organization, such as a *bond*; the holder of the bond is entitled to interest on the amount loaned, and the redemption of the bond by the borrower by repayment of the amount of the loan

deductions [tax] business or personal expenses that may be subtracted from gross income to calculate net income

default omission or failure to perform a legal duty, such as the repayment of a loan when due

deferred contribution payments that are either postponed or made in installments

depreciation [tax] reduction of worth or lessening of value of property from age; calculated by approved IRS formulas

dissolution cancellation or abrogation of an agreement (i.e., a contract) by the affected parties; the termination of a business with the liquidation of the business's assets

doing-business-as name used when conducting a business or sole proprietorship under a name other than under the owners' names; requires local or state registration; also known as DBA (see also *fictitious business name*)

domestic corporation term used within a state to describe a corporation formed within that state, contrasted to a *foreign corporation* formed in another state

domicile true, fixed, and permanent home and principal establishment

EIN see *employer identification number*

employer identification number number issued by state and federal governments to identify a business for tax purposes; also known as EIN

equity ownership investment in property

equity security document or other proof, such as a share of stock, as evidence of ownership in a corporation

exemptions [tax] items other than business deductions not subject to taxation

fair market value price property or other assets would command on the open market

fictitious business name another way to describe *doing-business-as* or *DBA*

fiduciary duties duties related to the handling of finances or property or other matters for the benefit of another person; implies a high degree of confidence and trust with *good faith*

fixed assets assets in place and essential to the continued operation of a business

foreign corporation term used within a state to describe a corporation formed in another state, in contrast to a *domestic corporation* formed within that state

freeze-out effort by majority shareholders in a corporation to increase their shares of ownership to the detriment of minor shareholders

gain tax term as measure of the increased value of an asset over its original value upon transfer to new ownership

general partner see *general partnership*

general partnership business form in which two or more individuals or business organizations agree to operate a business together; principals in the general partnership are general partners

golden parachute employment contractual agreement to pay the employee a premium if the company undergoes a significant change in ownership and control; limited to three times salary if it is to be a deductible expense for the company

good faith honesty of intention

goodwill value placed on a business that is greater than the combination of capital, stocks, funds, and property; based on a positive attitude toward the business by the business's public

gross income [tax] total income received before deductions for expenses and other expenditures

injunction legal prohibition of a specific act by a person or that person's agent

intangible assets business values such as *goodwill*, *trademark*, *copyright*, or franchise

intellectual property general term used to describe *copyright, patent, trademark,* and *trade secrets*

inter vires within a corporation's legal power to act

joint and several liability the legal responsibility of one or more or all the parties to a liability (such as partners in a partnership) for the total amount of that liability

joint ventures association of two or more persons or businesses to combine property, monies, effects, skills and/or knowledge to carry out a single business enterprise for profit

Keogh plan tax-deferring retirement savings plan; also known as HR 10

key person insurance insurance policy taken out by a company on the life of a key person, such as an executive, to help weather the replacement transition when the key person dies

leverage debt where the creation of the debt creates more business or income than it costs

liability potentially subject to an obligation arising from a loss or damage resulting from a contingency, risk, or casualty

license certificate or document giving permission or authority for a defined action

limited liability limitation of responsibility for damages or losses; found in *limited partnerships* and through the *corporate shield*

limited partnership special form of *partnership* in which investors (limited partners) participate in profits and losses, but management of the partnership is by a *general partner*

litigation contest in a court of law to enforce a right or claim; a lawsuit

loss tax term indicating the dimunition in value of an asset from its original value on transfer to new ownership

Model Business Corporation Act overall "suggested" corporation statute approved by the Committee on Corporate Laws of the American Bar Association, with the latest changes made in 1991; many of the sections of this Act have been adopted with modifications in many of the 50 states

net profits what remains from *gross income* after deductions for business expenses and losses

nonprofit corporation sometimes called not-for-profit or public-service corporations; primary purpose is to provide a service rather than to generate a profit

notice information derived by the senses or the mind, or by communication from another person; knowledge of a fact or state of affairs (see also *constructive notice*)

oral agreements unwritten ("handshake") contractual agreements between parties; difficult to prove during lawsuits

partnership form of unincorporated business where two or more parties (individuals or organizations) agree to operate a business together

passive income/loss income or loss from investments or other sources without active participation (see *active income*)

patent a grant of specified privilege, property, or authority by a government body, such as the United States Patent and Trademark Office; a form of *intellectual property*

personal holding corporation corporation that derives 60% or more of its income from *passive income/loss*

personal service corporation organization formed to provide personal services in contrast to the manufacture and sale of products; see also *professional corporation*

preemptive right shareholder's right to purchase new shares of stock in the corporation before these shares are offered for sale to other purchasers

preferred stock shares held by "preferred" shareholders, which are paid at a guaranteed and fixed dividend in advance of dividend payments to others (e.g., common stock shareholders)

professional corporation organization formed to provide professional services, such as by doctors, lawyers, or architects

property appreciation see *appreciation*

property depreciation see *depreciation*

proxy a person who is substituted for or deputized by another to represent and act for the deputizing person, particularly in some meeting or public body, as to vote shares at an annual shareholder's meeting

public corporation see C *corporation*

quorum majority of the whole body, as a committee; can be a simple majority or, by agreement, a supermajority requiring a number greater than a simple majority

S corporation election by shareholders for a special form of corporation under Subchapter S of the tax code; profits and losses pass directly to the corporate *shareholders*

sanctions penalty or punishment to enforce obedience to a law

Section 1244 stock special Internal Revenue Code classification for small business stock that allows a greater portion than normal of corporate losses to pass through to the shareholders to apply against personal income from other sources

securities evidence of debt, rights, or property ownership, such as shares of stock

service business business formed to provide a service rather than a product

shareholder owner of a piece of a business, normally evidenced by a stock certificate

shareholder agreement agreement between two or more shareholders to vote their shares in a specified manner

sole proprietorship unincorporated business owned and directed by a single person

stock subscription agreement in advance of incorporation to purchase a stated number of shares at a stated price once incorporation has been completed

thin corporation corporation with a large amount of debt compared with money raised by the sale of stock

trademark distinctive mark of authenticity to distinguish one product source from another; can be registered for protection; another form of *intellectual property*

trade secrets plan, process, mechanism, procedure, or information used in business and known only to its owner; another form of *intellectual property*

trust accounts money controlled by one party (the trustee) for the benefit of another; see also *fiduciary duties*

ultra vires beyond the authority or power of the corporation

voting trust the transfer of voting rights by shareholders to the trustee of a voting trust, to be voted by the trustee

watered stock shares of stock having an actual value less than the stated value that are exchanged for the receipt of property

SECTION II

BECOMING A CORPORATION

CHAPTER 3

MAKING YOUR PLANS

WHICH TYPE OF CORPORATION?

As noted in Chapter 1, you can choose from several types of corporation, each with its own characteristics, and each of potential interest for small businesses.

Public (or "C") Corporation

This is what most people think of when they think of incorporation. This is a standard form, relatively nonrestrictive, which has the basic characteristics and advantages of the corporate form. The general public may own, sell, or purchase shares of common stock, which generally is traded through a stock exchange or some version of over-the-counter market.

While the C corporation carries the burden of double taxation of profits, its advantage over the S corporation is that a number of tax-deductible fringe benefits are allowed to the C corporation that are not allowed to the S corporation.

S (or Subchapter S) Corporation

This is a special variation of the C corporation with stringent restrictions on ownership. The S corporation was made a part of the Internal Revenue Code (IRC) in an effort to encourage small businesses. The S corporation has pass-through of profits and losses; that is, the corporation itself is not taxed.

While profits and losses of the S corporation pass directly to the shareholders for application in their personal tax returns without double taxation as with the C corporation, your corporation will be limited in the fringe benefits that may be deducted as operating expenses, such as medical and health insurance coverage.

Personal Service Corporation (or PSC)

In this special form of corporation, the stated purpose is to provide a service rather than to manufacture or sell goods. This form of incorporation is popular among professionals in states that require licensing, as for doctors, dentists, lawyers, or architects. In such cases, it is called a *professional corporation* or *professional association* and is usually designated as PC (for Professional Corporation) or PA (for Professional Association).

Ownership in the PSC is limited to persons licensed in the same licensed specialty, and shares can only be sold to those in the same licensed specialty. A major advantage when compared with a partnership is that one professional within the PSC is not liable for the negligence of an associate; a shareholder is responsible for only his or her own negligence or the negligence of those under the shareholder's control or supervision.

Closely Held Corporation

This is also called a close corporation, closed corporation, or private corporation; it includes the S corporation. In the closely held corporation, the total ownership of the corporation is within a small group, such as a family, and there is no public marketing of stock. Except for the fact of narrow ownership, this type of corporation does not differ from a C Corporation.

Personal Holding Corporation (or PHC)

This Internal Revenue Service (IRS) designation is used to discourage incorporated "pocketbooks" from accumulating excessive amounts of passive income, such as from royalties, investment interest and dividends, annuities, personal-service contracts, or rentals. The PHC is usually formed by a talented person with a modest salary draw, allowing the accumulation of funds to anticipate lesser earnings in the future.

The IRS has two tests for a PHC, either of which confirms its existence: (1) more than 50% of the fair market value of the outstanding stock is owned by five or fewer individuals at any time during the last half of the tax year, and (2) in the tainted income test, 60% or more of the adjusted ordinary gross income (excluding capital gains) is derived from personal PHC income.

PLANNING AHEAD

A number of things necessary to the successful launch of your corporation business must be addressed before actual incorporation. If more than one person is to be involved in the incorporation, the most important item is the *Preincorporation Agreement*. Even if you are to be the sole incorporator, the factors considered in the Preincorporation Agreement should be worked out in detail before you take the plunge.

THE PREINCORPORATION AGREEMENT

The idea of the Preincorporation Agreement (PA) is to outline your business, its objectives, and its methods in advance. And, if more than one person is involved, the agreement assures that there is a meeting of the minds—a mutual understanding of what is to be done, how it is to be done, and by whom it will be done.

Preamble

The PA should begin with the statement that those persons signing the PA (in essence a contract) intend to form a corporation under the laws of a specified state.

Corporate Name

What's in a name? A great deal. The name you select for your corporation may have a very positive influence on how successful your business will be. But you won't be entirely free in your selection of a name.

Most state laws require that your corporation name identify that it is a corporation by including the words *corporation*, *incorporated*, or *limited* (or the abbreviations *corp.*, *inc.*, or *ltd.*) as a part of the corporation's name. Most states have a provision for reserving a name for a specified time while you are getting your organization under way.

The name you choose cannot be the same as or closely resemble that of another corporation in the state, or in any other way create a *confusion of source* to the public. Unfortunately, there is no national registry to prevent confusion or similarities to names of corporations in other states. There are safeguards, however. If you were in the computer business and you tried to name your corporation IBM (for, say, Inter-Byte Modems), IBM would most likely take you to court to prevent the use of the IBM acronym.

You may be prevented from using your own name for the corporation, if it too would cause confusion of source. If your name were Estee Lauder, for example, the famous Estee Lauder could take you to court to prevent your use of that name as your business name.

Other statutory restrictions are aimed preventing names that might suggest erroneously that the corporation is a governmental agency, a bank, an insurance company, a charity, a religious organization, and such. And, of course, you will be prevented from using a profanity or vulgarity as your corporation name.

If you plan to do business in (that is, more than just sell to) other states in addition to the state in which you are incorporated, you will have to file with that other state as a *foreign* (out-of-state) corporation. If there is a confusion of names, you might find it advisable or necessary to file a *fictitious name* for your operations in that state.

Corporate Purpose

What is to be the purpose of your business? How detailed is your business plan? A business plan can be simple or complex. What is most important is that you end up with a reasonably complete picture of your overall objectives as well as specific estimates of your sales potential and revenues; in short, the plan should indicate the direction you will take and its overall feasibility.

It is the business plan that will give you a sense of direction. It will be the culmination of your thoughts and plans (and those of the others who work with you during the planning phase). It will contain clear statements of what you intend to do, your goals and targets, benchmarks along the way, strategies and tactics, programs, schedules, and policies.

Perhaps of equal importance, the business plan will give you a head start when you approach a lender for operating funds or an investor for the sale of shares of stock. The elements of building and using your business plan can be found in *Contracting Your Services,* by Robert L. Davidson, III (John Wiley & Sons).

Registered Office and Agent

You will be required to give the name of an agent and an address within the state where you incorporate. The purpose is to provide a name and address where you can receive communications from the state government and others. This does not need to be your company headquarters address, and it can be changed at any time by filing notice of change with the state government, usually the office of the state's secretary of state.

You or any other of those who will incorporate the business, or a complete outsider, can be the agent. You can hire someone for the role, or you can have your attorney or accountant serve as your agent.

Corporate Capitalization

How will you fund the business? Do you and your coincorporators have the money? Will you raise money by selling shares of stock in the business? Will you sell to family and friends, or try to sell to a broader public? Or will you borrow from a bank or other lending institution?

First, how much do you need to start up? How much will you need to keep operating until your income equals or exceeds your outgo? To answer these questions, you must have a business plan, as discussed earlier. You must know what expenses you will have, what product or service you will be selling, how you can price your product or service, and how many or how much you must sell.

Authorization for Capital Stock

Now is the time to decide how much capital stock will be authorized when you incorporate. And of the stock that will be authorized, how much of it will the incorporators subscribe to (see "Subscription Agreement," later in this chapter). How much will be held by the corporation for future sale or other distribution?

Names of Incorporators

The process of incorporation can be handled by a single person or a group of people. The incorporator(s) do not need to be future shareholders of the corporation, nor do they need to have any other role in the corporation once the incorporation is completed.

In general, the incorporator can be a natural person or another corporation, either domestic or foreign. The incorporator does not have to be a resident of the state. This means that you can incorporate in any state, regardless of where you live, just as long as there is an agent and a registered office in the state in which you incorporate.

Voting Rights for Shareholders

A simple ownership structure most likely will have one vote per share. More complicated structures with different classes, each with a different voting authority, may follow at some future date as your corporation grows and becomes more complex. Other future items to consider will be *shareholder agreements* or *voting trusts.*

Since the primary authority of a shareholder is to vote for the members of the board of directors, you will want to define what you mean by *quorum* and *majority.* A quorum for voting purposes can be whatever you wish, with representation of less than half of the shares, to a simple quorum of the shares, to a superquorum of, for example, two thirds or three quarters.

For the voting itself, you can require a simple majority of the shares voted when a quorum is present, or, as for the quorum, a supermajority. Voting can be straight or can be cumulative allowing each voter to cast all votes for a single director, or one vote for each directorship opening.

Preemptive Rights Given

The presence of a preemptive right gives the holders of small numbers of shares protection against an attempted freeze-out by holders of large numbers of shares. This means that whenever the corporation (that is, the board of directors) votes to issue more shares for sale, every present shareholder has the first right to buy new shares in proportion to his or her present ownership. Should this right be ignored by the small shareholder, that person's proportion of ownership in the corporation will be even smaller.

Indemnification of Directors and Officers

The so-called business-judgment rule normally protects a director or an officer against financial liability for mistakes of judgment made in good faith. Even so, the accused person may be saddled with very large legal-defense fees. Will you indemnify (that is, "make whole" financially) such persons for their legal expenses? What if the director or officer is accused of wrongdoing and convicted? Many states do allow a corporation to carry insurance for this purpose.

Board of Directors

Who will be on your board of directors, the group that sets policies for the corporation and elects (or dismisses) the officers of the corporation? How many directors will you have? Note that a director does not have to be a shareholder of the corporation nor an officer, but can be both.

Initial Shareholders

Who will be the initial owners, that is the shareholders, for the new corporation? (See "Subscription Agreement," at the end of this chapter).

Section 1244 Stock

The Internal Revenue Code in Section 1244 has a special provision for shareholders of small businesses where the stock loses its value. Normally, your loss on the sale or exchange of worthless stock is treated as a capital loss, and $3,000 at most of the loss can be applied against ordinary personal income.

In Section 1244, a domestic small-business corporation may issue stock that qualifies as 1244 stock where up to $50,000 ($100,000 for married couples reporting on a joint return) of any loss through sale, exchange, or worthlessness can be applied against ordinary personal income. To qualify:

1. The small-business corporation's equity capital cannot exceed $1 million.
2. The stock must be issued for money, property, other stock, or securities.
3. The corporation must be actively engaged in a trade or business.
4. The holder of the stock must have been an original holder of the stock, that is, from the date of issuance.
5. The stock cannot have been issued to a corporation, trust, or estate.
6. Corporate gross receipts must not have exceeded 50% from passive income (e.g., interest, dividends, rentals, annuities, royalties) during the five tax years before the loss.

Power of Board of Directors to Act

How much power do you want to give to the Board of Directors? This power can be constrained in favor of the shareholders, if so desired and so stated in the Articles of Incorporation. If there are only a few shareholders, you might want to have the shareholders elect or dismiss the officers of the corporation, instead of giving this power to the directors.

Noncompete Covenant

Both the directors and officers owe a fiduciary (in trust) duty of care and loyalty to the corporation and its shareholders, and are required to act in the best interests of the corporation using that degree of care in the management of the business that would be used by ordinary and prudent people in similar circumstances.

This means that there should be no conflict of interests between the directors or officers and the corporation. No one should be serving their own interests at the expense of the corporation. Sometimes, however, it is good policy to spell out this duty and loyalty with a noncompete clause. While it does not add to the burden of duty and loyalty, it does remind all concerned to avoid conflicts of interest.

Other Items to Consider

Other items that should be considered and included in the Preincorporation Agreement include:

- What kind of expenses will be reimbursable by the corporation?
- Where will the principal office be located?
- Who will hold what office in the corporation?
- How will you resolve disagreements (e.g., mediation, arbitration)?
- Who will be paid what as a corporation employee?
- What fringe benefits will the corporation provide?

WARNING: Don't trap yourself or your corporation-to-be at this time with firm commitments to suppliers. You'll need to know what your business expenses will be, but if your corporation does not become a reality, or if your plans change, you don't want to be locked into an undesired agreement at this time.

The information you develop and the decisions you make in creating the Preincorporation Agreement will be used later when you prepare your Articles of Incorporation and bylaws.

SUBSCRIPTION AGREEMENT

Prior to starting your business, it is important to know the sources of support you will have, particularly in the sale of shares of stock. This support, shown by agreements to purchase stock in the corporation once incorporation is completed, should be recorded in an enforceable written and signed contract including all persons active in the planning of the business.

The contract should be specific as to who will purchase shares, how many each person will purchase, and the price that they will pay for the shares. The contract should clearly state the period during which it is irrevocable (e.g., six months) and the penalties for those who violate the terms of the contract.

Questions to decide include these: What kind of payment will be acceptable? Money? Property? Services? Equipment? What else? How will nonmoney payments be valued? When services are traded for stock, the services must be performed prior to the distribution of the stock; they cannot be future services or promissory notes.

CHAPTER 4

YOUR ARTICLES AND BYLAWS

GETTING STARTED

In this chapter, you will see how to prepare your Articles of Incorporation and bylaws, and how to conduct the Organizational Meeting (the first official meeting of the incorporators) and the first meeting of the board of directors.

ARTICLES OF INCORPORATION

The Articles of Incorporation (or Articles), sometimes called the Certificate of Incorporation, is what you file with the state (normally with the state's secretary of state) to effect your incorporation. While each state has its own requirements, in general the Articles you file will contain the following elements:

1. *Name of Corporation* (discussed in Chapter 3).
2. *Street Address.* You must give an actual address; a post office box is not enough.
3. *Corporate Purpose.* Your statement of corporate purpose can be narrow and specific, or broad and all encompassing. It is best not to fence yourself in at so early a stage. Consider: "The purpose of this corporation is to conduct any legally permissible business for profit."
4. *Registered Office and Agent.* This was discussed in Chapter 3 under "The Preincorporation Agreement." You must have a registered office and agent where state and federal agencies can make written contact with your corporation. You can name yourself and your home address, or you can specify anyone else, but the person must reside in the state in which you have incorporated.
5. *Names and Addresses of Incorporators.* One or more persons can be the incorporators (either natural persons or domestic or foreign corporations). Incorporation is purely a procedure, and the incorporator or incorporators do not need to be owners or employees of the corporation.

6. *Names and Addresses of Initial Board of Directors.* Normally three directors are required, unless, of course, the corporation is to have a single owner and single employee. These initial directors are temporary, and may, if so desired, be replaced by permanent directors at the organizational meeting.
7. *Authorized Capital.* How much stock will be issued? Classes? Par value (or no par)?

Other items you may wish to have in your Articles, but usually are not required, include:

- Preemptive rights for shareholders.
- Stock transfer restrictions, if any.
- Voting requirements per share if there are to be voting-class differences.
- Board of directors' authority to fix compensation.
- Whether board meetings are to be in person, by phone, or other provisions.
- Indemnification for directors and officers.
- Provisions for cumulative voting.
- Provisions for removal of directors.

Items you cannot decree in your Articles are those that would prevent shareholders from voting on the amendment of the Articles, or on a merger, consolidation, or transfer of substantially all the corporate assets.

Normally, corporate life begins on receipt of the Articles by the state secretary of state.

Several sample Articles and Certificates of Incorporation are shown in Appendix II.

ORGANIZATIONAL MEETING

The *Organizational Meeting*, the first official meeting of the incorporators, is called and held as soon as practical after filing of the Articles. Most often, there is a *waiver of notice* of the meeting (see Appendix II) so that the meeting is not delayed. Written minutes of this meeting, and of all subsequent meetings of shareholders and directors, must be taken and maintained, telling when and where the meeting was held, who attended (and who was absent), who chaired the meeting, and who was secretary. A typical sequence of actions at such a meeting is:

1. The meeting is called to order.
2. The chairperson reports that the Articles were filed on a certain date.
3. The chairperson directs that a copy of the Articles (or Certificate of Incorporation) be inserted into the minutes book as part of the official record of the meeting.
4. A proposed form of the bylaws (assuming that they are now ready) is read and, if approved (or as amended), is adopted and directed to be made a part of the permanent record.

5. The permanent board of directors is elected, replacing the temporary board of directors listed in the Articles. These may be the same directors, or a completely new group.
6. Any other business, such as a discussion of facilities or insurance, or whatever, is brought up, discussed, and either acted on, tabled, or delegated.
7. The meeting is adjourned.

What if you were the sole incorporator as well as the sole shareholder? Then you would file a statement in the minutes book, in lieu of the Organizational Meeting.

FIRST MEETING OF THE BOARD OF DIRECTORS

With the election of the board of directors in the Organizational Meeting, the corporation is ready for business. The first step is for the board of directors to meet. As for the Organizational Meeting, it is most likely that there will be a *waiver of notice* (see Appendix II) so that important early business of the corporation will not be delayed.

As before, there will be written minutes of the meeting with information on place, date, attendance, who chaired and who was secretary. This same pattern is to be followed for all subsequent meetings of the board. A typical sequence of activities at this meeting would be:

1. Meeting is called to order by the chairperson.
2. Officers (president, vice president, secretary, treasurer) will be nominated, discussed, and voted on. Note: in a very small business, there can be duplication of offices, but normally it is not permissible for one person to be both president and secretary.
3. The corporate seal and stock certificate (assuming that they have already been designed) are voted on, and, if accepted, will be approved.
4. A vote will be taken on who is to serve as the corporation's registered agent, and at what address.
5. A vote will be taken on the location of the corporate bank account.
6. A vote will be taken to authorize the treasurer to pay all fees and expenses incident to the incorporation.
7. Shareholder contributions will be accepted for their shares, according to their commitments in the Subscription Agreement (see Chapter 4).
8. A possible decision will be made on the desirability of a S corporation election.
9. Fringe benefits programs may be discussed and planned.
10. A fiscal year (tax year) will be adopted.
11. The principal office location may be designated at this time.

The directors then sign (ratify and approve) the minutes and the decisions made during the meeting. If the bylaws are ready, they may be approved at this meeting. If is assumed here that by the preparation of the Preincorporation Agreement and the

Subscription Agreement, potential problems were eliminated or negotiated prior to this meeting, thus avoiding delays and unexpected disagreements at this early stage of the business.

OTHER EARLY ACTIONS

There are other actions and decisions to consider at this time, or, if not now, in very short order. The two most important and most immediate actions you should take are:

- Apply for your EIN (Employer's Identification Number) using Form SS-4 (see Appendix I). You must have this number to identify your corporation for both federal and state tax records and other official documents.
- Apply for and obtain necessary local occupancy and business permits, and apply for and obtain necessary licenses to conduct your type of business.

Other actions that you should take early in the life of your corporation and that you should have studied during your work on the Preincorporation Agreement or, if you are alone in the business, in your business plan, include the following:

- *Obtain Worker's (or Workman's) Compensation Insurance.* This is mandatory in most states if you plan to have employees. If only yourself or your family, or independent contractors, will do the work of the corporation, you may consider skipping this step. Discuss it with your attorney or insurance broker.
- *Contract for Key Person Life Insurance.* This is the type of life insurance you buy for persons who are so important to your business that it will be difficult and time consuming to replace them in case of their death. The payoff from the insurance is meant to either fill in the income-loss gap or cover the expenses of finding a replacement.
- *Look to Employee Benefit Plans.* You may not be ready for this step so early in the life of your corporation. Benefit plans, particularly those that involve medical insurance, can be expensive and burdensome for a freshly formed business. On the other hand, you will want some forms of protection, such as medical insurance or a retirement plan, for yourself and perhaps family members active in the corporation.
- *Obtain Liability Insurance.* If you are an attorney or a doctor, you are already quite familiar with malpractice (liability) insurance. Even if your business is quite simple and is offering a basic service, there is always the risk of damage to property or injury to people, customers, and innocent bystanders, for example, from the simple act of driving your car to the site of a work contract. The amount of liability insurance you will need will be directly related to the type of product or service your business will be offering. Discuss this with your insurance broker.
- *Consider Other Types of Insurance.* Consider also property insurance to cover losses to your facilities and its contents, particularly buildings, furniture, computers, tools, equipment, or supplies. Consider also business interruption

insurance to keep you solvent while you rebuild or remodel, or recover from other interruptions caused by weather, road reconstruction, riots, and so on.

- Make an S corporation election using Form 2553 (see Appendix I). You do not, of course, have to make the S corporation election, but if you wish to do so, your business must first be incorporated as a C corporation.

CORPORATION BYLAWS

Your corporation's bylaws are the rules and regulations under which it is to operate. Your bylaws describe power in the corporation: where it is, who has it, how it is used, and how it is controlled, tailored to your specific needs. While bylaws do not need to be officially filed with any state or local official or agency, they do become "law" internally. A detailed example of a sample set of bylaws is presented in Appendix II.

You are allowed a great deal of flexibility in the drafting of your bylaws, but their authority is not unlimited. They must be consistent with state laws and federal tax statutes, and they cannot contradict your Articles of Incorporation. Note: If you do want a provision in your bylaws, and you cannot because of a provision in your Articles, you can amend your Articles. See Appendix II for a sample of a form used for such a purpose.

Your board of directors, or you by yourself if you are the only director, will be responsible for drafting and adopting the corporation's bylaws. In truth, you should by this time already have the bylaws drafted or be fully aware of what will be in them, the result of your earlier preincorporation planning. Once drafted and adopted, the bylaws can be amended or repealed by the board of directors.

Following are the major elements found in most bylaws:

- *Offices.* Give the registered agent and the agent's location; give the board authority to change the agent or the address, or both. Give the principal or headquarters office, with authority to make changes and to establish additional offices.
- *Shareholders.* Give a general description of rules and procedures regulating shareholder meetings (when, where, notice for) and voting (straight or cumulative, etc.). Provisions for the calling of and conducting special meetings of shareholders, either by the shareholders themselves, or by the board include:

  What kind of notice, and when, for meetings.

  Who can vote; when they must be listed as shareholders.

  What constitutes a quorum for voting.

  Whether or not proxy voting is allowed, and any restrictions.

  Whether or not shareholder action can be taken in writing only.
- *Directors.* Give listing of duties and responsibilities of the directors, the number of directors, how elected (e.g., at shareholder meetings or by unanimous written consent of shareholders). Items to include:

  Whether they must be residents of the state.

  Powers to manage affairs of the corporation.

  Policy-making powers.

Authority to appoint or remove corporation officers, unless this power is reserved for the shareholders.

Restrictions as to conflicts of interest or competition with the corporation.

Regular meeting frequency, and notice for meetings.

Special meetings, called by whom, notice.

What constitutes a quorum (majority or supermajority).

Majority or supermajority vote by attendees.

Provisions for or against voting by proxy.

How directorship vacancies are to be filled.

Authority to delegate work to committees.

How a director can be removed.

Who sets compensation for directors; how much.

Whether or not directors will be indemnified; if so, for what.

- *Officers.* What positions, such as president, vice president, treasurer, secretary. Whether or not one person can serve in more than one position (the Model Business Corporation Act prohibits a single person serving as both president and secretary; check for the law of your state). Duties, responsibilities, and authorities for each of the titles. Other items include:

  Whether or not officers also can be directors.

  Whether or not there will be term limits with reappointment or replacements by the directors.

  How officers are selected (by shareholders or by directors).

  Provisions for and restrictions to fault or no-fault removal of officers.

  Provisions for employment contracts with officers.

  Provisions for severance pay and/or golden parachutes.

  Provisions for compensation, including bonuses and stock options.

  Whether or not officers will be indemnified; if so, for what.

- *Financial.* Who among the various officers of the corporation will have what financial authority, such as:

  Signing of contracts, and dollar limits.

  Who has authority to borrow or lend.

  Who has check-signing authority.

  Which bank and which branch will be used.

  Who will keep the financial records.

  Who will audit the financial records annually.

- *Other Items.* Here are other items for the bylaws:

  Statement of the fiscal (tax and accounting) year.

  Corporate seal design and modification.

  Procedure to amend the bylaws.

SECTION III

RUNNING YOUR CORPORATION

CHAPTER 5

YOUR CORPORATION AND TAXES

YOU AND THE INTERNAL REVENUE SERVICE

As a corporation, you will be held responsible for a number of tax returns on federal, state, and sometimes municipal levels. Since state and municipal tax requirements vary widely, only federal tax reporting will be covered here. Your tax advisor or accountant can help you plan for state and local tax record keeping and reporting.

The IRS flings a broad net when it defines the word *corporation* for tax purposes; namely, a corporation includes associations, joint stock companies, insurance companies, trusts, and partnerships that actually operate as associations or corporations. Also included are organizations of doctors, lawyers, and other professional people organized under state professional association acts or corporate statutes *if* they are both organized and operated as corporations.

Even unincorporated organizations are taxed as though they are corporations if they are organized to carry on business, divide the gains from the business, and have a majority of the following characteristics:

- Continuity of life.
- Centralization of management.
- Limited liability.
- Free transferability of interests.

In preparing for your tax returns, several IRS publications will be most helpful to you. Appendix III, "Helpful Tax Publications," tells you how to get copies of these publications. In brief, they are:

- Publication 535: *Business Expenses;* details on deductions.
- Publication 536: *Net Operating Losses;* calculation and carryover of losses.
- Publication 538: *Accounting Periods and Methods;* accounting periods and tax years.

- Publication 542: *Tax Information on Corporations;* figuring the tax.
- Publication 551: *Basis of Assets;* valuation of business property, stocks, and bonds.
- Publication 925: *Passive Activity and At-Risk Rules;* limits to passive income, identifying at-risk situations.
- Publication 937: *Business Reporting;* employment taxes and information returns.

EMPLOYMENT TAXES—WITHHOLDING RULES

Your first chore is to define which of the persons performing services for you are employees and which are independent contractors. There are significant differences in keeping records for and paying taxes for employees as opposed to independent contractors. The IRS (Publication 937) categories are:

1. *An Independent Contractor.* In general, persons performing services for you for pay are independent contractors if you as employer control or direct *only* the result of the work, not the means and methods of accomplishing the result.
2. *A Common-Law Employee.* When you as employer have the right (even though not exercised) to tell a person performing services for you what means and methods to use, the IRS may categorize that person as an employee for taxation purposes, even though both you and that person deem him or her to be an independent contractor.
3. *A Statutory Employee.* This includes anyone working for you as a driver distributing certain products, a full-time life insurance agent, a person working at home with materials or goods you provide and which must be returned to you or someone you designate, if you also provide specifications for the work to be done.
4. *A Statutory Nonemployee.* This covers direct sellers who sell or solicit sales of consumer products, but not in a permanent retail establishment, and licensed real estate agents.

For independent contractors, you do not have to withhold income tax or social security tax (FICA); the independent contractor will do this independently of you. If, however, you pay the independent contractor $600 or more during the year, you must file a Form 1099-MISC, *Statement for Recipients of Miscellaneous Income,* shown in Appendix I.

For common-law employees, you may have to withhold income tax and social security tax (FICA) from the wages you pay. You may also have to pay federal unemployment tax (FUTA) and your share of social security (FICA) on these taxes.

For statutory employees, you do not have to withhold income tax. You must, however, withhold and pay social security (FICA) taxes. Unless they are full-time life insurance sales agents or work at home, you must also pay the federal unemployment tax (FUTA) on their wages.

For statutory nonemployees, you have no withholding duties.

TAXES AND "BUYING" STOCK—DEFINITION OF TERMS

The IRS looks to gain or loss when deciding if a transfer of corporation stock to you is taxable. *Gain* or *loss* for tax purposes for a transfer of property in exchange for stock is determined by comparing the *adjusted basis* of the transferred property with its *fair market value* at the time of transfer.

If you transfer money or property in return for stock in the corporation and immediately have 80% control of the corporation, for tax purposes neither you nor the corporation recognizes a gain or loss. However, if you transfer your services to the corporation in return for stock, the stock is considered income to you and is taxable to you, as well as being a tax deduction to the corporation. If the property you transfer to the corporation is mortgaged, there may be a taxable gain if the liabilities assumed by the corporation exceed the adjusted basis of the property.

The *adjusted basis* of stock received by you in exchange for property is the same as the basis of the property you transferred for the stock decreased by the fair market value of any other property you receive, the amount of money you receive, and any loss to you by the exchange, increased by any amount treated as a dividend and any gain you recognized by the exchange.

The adjusted basis to the corporation of the stock transferred to you in exchange for 80% control of the corporation, where you had no gain or loss, is the same for the corporation as it was for you, adjusted for any property you receive along with the transfer.

START-UP EXPENSES

While you cannot make an immediate business deduction for start-up expenses, you can amortize them over a period of not less than 60 months if you treat such expenses as deferred expenses.

Don't confuse start-up expenses discussed here with organizational expenses discussed in the next section. A start-up expense is one that you pay or incur before your business starts operation; those expenses to create an active trade or business, or to investigate the possibility of creating or acquiring an active trade or business. Examples include:

- Survey of potential markets.
- Analysis of available facilities, labor supply, and so on.
- Advertisements for the opening of your business.
- Salaries or wages to train employees and for their trainers.
- Travel and related expenses to line up distributors, suppliers, or customers.
- Salaries or fees for executives, consultants, or other professional services.

ORGANIZATIONAL EXPENSES

You can deduct organizational expenses in equal monthly amounts over a period of not less than 60 months, starting with the first month the corporation is actively engaged in business, that is, when you actually start the activities for which you are organized.

Organizational expenses are those directly connected with the creation of the corporation that would be chargeable to the capital account. They include:

- Expenses of temporary directors.
- Expenses of meetings of temporary directors or shareholders.
- Fees paid to a state for incorporation.
- Accounting expenses and legal expenses incident to organization, such as to draft the charter, bylaws, minutes of organizational meetings, and terms of the original stock certificates.

You cannot deduct or amortize expenses for issuing or selling stock or securities, such as commissions, professional fees, and printing costs. Nor can you deduct or amortize expenses connected with the transfer of assets to the corporation.

GOLDEN PARACHUTE PAYMENTS

Although you may not connect the idea of a *golden parachute* with a newly organized small-business corporation, you may find that a person who will be key to the success of your business will want such protection before joining. A golden parachute is an agreement to make a payment to the person concerned if there is a major or substantial change in the ownership of the corporation.

The tax rule for golden parachute payments is that if, when made, they exceed three times the recipient's base compensation amount, the excess of any golden parachute payment over the portion of the base amount allocated to the payment is not deductible.

CHARITABLE CONTRIBUTIONS

Your corporation may claim deductions for charitable contributions that do not exceed 10% of your taxable income. If the 10% limit is exceeded, you may be allowed to carry over the excess amount to each of the following five years.

To be deductible, the contribution must be made to or for the use of community chests, funds, foundations, corporations, or trusts organized and operated *exclusively* for religious, charitable, scientific, literary, or educational purposes, or to foster national or international amateur sports competition, or for the prevention of cruelty to children or animals, or for other charitable organizations.

The deduction will not be allowed if any of the net earnings of the recipient organization are used to benefit a private shareholder or individual, so be careful where you place your charitable donations.

FIGURING THE TAX

In figuring your tax at the end of your tax year, you first must calculate your net income or net loss. This is done by subtracting operating costs and other allowable deductions (listed under "What You Can Deduct," later in this chapter) from your gross income.

At-Risk Limitations

Be aware that losses will be limited by the IRS's *at-risk rules* for any activity as a trade or business, or for a closely held corporation. You cannot declare a loss that is greater than the amount you have at risk (what you can lose), namely:

1. The money and the adjusted basis of the property you have contributed to the activity, and
2. Amounts you borrow for use in the activity, if:
   a. You are personally liable for repayment, or
   b. You pledge property not used in the activity as security for the loan.

Corporate Tax Rate

Corporate taxable income is subject to tax under a three-bracket graduated rate system:

Taxable Income	*Tax Rate*
Not over $50,000	15%
Over $50,000, not over $75,000	25%
Over $75,000	34%

An additional 5% tax, up to $11,750, is imposed on corporate taxable income over $100,000. Corporations with taxable incomes of at least $335,000 pay a flat rate of 34%.

Taxable incomes of qualified personal service corporations (including professional service corporations) are taxed at a flat rate of 34%. The IRS defines a qualified personal service corporation in terms of the following attributes:

- At least 95% of the value of its stock is held by employees, or heir estates or beneficiaries.
- Its employees perform services at least 95% of the time in any of the following fields:

  Health
  Law
  Engineering
  Architecture
  Accounting
  Actuarial science
  Performing arts
  Consulting

Other Taxes

Other taxes you may have to consider include:

- Personal holding company tax (Schedule PH, Form 1120).
- Investment credit recapture.

- Alternative minimum tax.
- Environmental tax.

Alternative Minimum Tax

If your corporation qualifies for a large number of tax credits and special deductions, the tax law provides that you will pay at the very least a minimum tax. This is called the *alternative minimum tax* and is calculated and reported using Form 4626, *Alternative Minimum Tax—Corporations.*

Tax Credits

Credits that can be used to reduce your tax liability include:

- Credit for fuels and lubricants used for certain purposes (see IRS Publication 378, *Fuel Tax Credits and Refunds*).
- Foreign tax credit (use Form 1118).
- General business credit (use Form 3800).
- Orphan drug credit (use Form 6765).
- Possessions tax credit (use Form 5735).
- Credit for fuel produced from a nonconventional source.

General business credit covers a number of areas figured separately on appropriate forms. These include investment credit (Form 3468), jobs credit (Form 5884), alcohol fuel credit (Form 6478), low-income housing credit (Form 8586), and research credit (Form 6765).

Filing Your Tax Return

Your taxes are reported on Form 1120, *U.S. Corporation Income Tax Return,* or Form 1120-A, *U.S. Corporation Short-Form Income Tax Return,* both of which are illustrated at the end of this chapter.

You will be able to have the convenience and simplicity of the Form 1120-A short form if your corporation meets all the following requirements:

- Gross receipts less than $500,000.
- Total income less than $500,000.
- Total assets less than $500,000.
- No ownership in a foreign corporation.
- No foreign shareholders who own directly or indirectly 50% or more of the stock.
- Not a member of a controlled group or a personal holding company.
- Not a consolidated corporate return filer.
- Not undergoing dissolution or liquidation.
- Not filing its final tax return.

- No refundable tax credits other than the general business credit and the credit for prior-year minimum tax.
- Dividend income only from domestic corporations and those dividends that qualify for the 80% (or 70%) deduction.
- Not an organization such as an S corporation, life or mutual insurance company, or political organization that is required to file a specialized form such as Form 1120S, 1120-L, or 1120-POL.
- No liability for interest relating to certain installment sales of timeshares and residential lots, or interest on deferred tax liability or installment payments of tax.
- Not subject to environmental law.

You can learn more on this subject from the IRS's "Instructions for Forms 1120 and 1120-A."

Schedules M-1, Part III, and M-2

If you file Form 1120, the last page contains Schedules M-1 and M-2. These must be completed if your total assets are at least $25,000. If, however, you are filing Form 1120-A, Part III must be filled in, regardless of your total assets.

WHAT YOU CAN DEDUCT

Business expenses are the normal and current costs of carrying on a trade, business, or profession. In general, these expenses can be deducted if they are both ordinary and necessary in a business operated to make a profit. For tax purposes, these expenses are divided into (1) those used to figure the cost of goods sold, and (2) capital expenses.

- *Cost of Goods Sold.* Included are the costs of raw materials in your inventory, including shipping costs; cost of storing products you sell; direct labor costs (including contributions to pension or annuity plans); depreciation on machinery used to produce the products; and factory overhead.
- *Capital Expenses.* Costs considered part of your investment in your business are called *capital expenses.* In general they include (1) going into business, (2) business assets, and (3) improvements.

Specific Deductions Allowed

You cannot deduct more for a business expense than the amount you actually spent. Otherwise, if the amount is reasonable, there is usually no limit on how much you can deduct. When you can make the deduction depends on the type of accounting system you use:

- *Cash Method of Accounting.* Under this system, business expenses are deducted in the tax year in which they were actually paid, even if the expense was incurred in a prior year.

- *Accrual Method of Accounting*. Under this system, you can deduct business expenses when you become liable for them, whether or not you pay them in that year.

Deducting Employee's Pay

To be deductible, an employee's pay must meet four basic tests:

- *Test 1: Ordinary and Necessary*. Directly connected with your trade or business.
- *Test 2: Reasonable*. The amount must be that which would ordinarily be paid for these services by like enterprises under similar circumstances.
- *Test 3: For Services Performed*. You must prove that the payment was for services actually performed. You can't, for example, pay your children a "salary" in return for nothing.
- *Test 4: Paid or Incurred*. You must have either paid the expense or incurred it during the tax year.

Other Deductions

- *Bonuses*. Allowable as deductions if they are intended as additional pay for services, not as gifts.
- *Gifts*. Deductible up to $25 per employee if used to promote employee goodwill.
- *Awards*. Employee achievement awards are deductible, subject to certain limits.
- *Loans*. Loans or advances made to an employee when you do not expect the employee to repay generally are deductible if they are for personal services actually performed.
- *Vacation Pay*. Includes what you pay for an employee on vacation, or amounts you pay when the employee chooses not to take a vacation. Such pay is deductible.
- *Unpaid Salaries*. Under a deferred salary payment plan, you can deduct the amount according to the type of accounting system you are using.
- *Meals and Lodging*. Generally, you can deduct the costs of furnishing meals and lodging to your employees (normally a maximum of 80%) for expenses that are ordinary and necessary business expenses.
- *Meals and Entertainment*. Generally, you can deduct only 80% of business-related meal and entertainment expenses incurred while traveling away from home on business, in entertaining business customers at your place of business or restaurant, or in attending a business convention or reception, business meeting, or business luncheon at a club.
- *Company Cafeteria or Executive Dining Room*. Normally, the deduction for this expense is limited to 80%.
- *Employee Activities*. Expenses of providing recreational, social, or similar activities, or the use of a facility by employees not highly paid, are deductible and not subject to the 80% limit.
- *Expenses Treated as Compensation*. You can deduct expenses for meals, goods, services, the use of a facility, or an allowance for meals and entertainment without the 80% limit if you treat the expense as compensation to the employee.

- *Employee's Reimbursed Expenses.* You can deduct up to 80% for expenses reimbursed to employees for business-related meal and entertainment expenses not treated as compensation.
- *Trade Association Meetings.* You can deduct expenses directly related to and necessary for attending business meetings or conventions, with the 80% limit.
- *De Minimis Fringe Benefits.* The 80% limit does not apply to an expense for food or beverages excludable from gross income that is so small in value that it would be unreasonable or impractical for you to account for it.
- *Group Term Life Insurance for Employees.* You can deduct group life insurance premiums paid for or incurred by you on policies covering the lives of your officers and employees if you are not directly or indirectly the beneficiary under the contract. For the employee, if the policy is in excess of $50,000, the additional premium you pay becomes income to the employee.
- *Education Expenses.* Payments for tuition for employees enrolled in courses not required for their job or not otherwise job related are treated as wages with the normal income tax, FICA, and FUTA withholding. As such they are business expenses.
- *Dependent Care Assistance Programs.* You can exclude up to $5,000 from an employee's gross income if you are paying for or providing child care or disabled dependent care services so that your employee can work.
- *Moving Expenses.* Payments to an employee for the cost of moving to a new job site are included in the employee's income but are not considered wages for purposes of withholding income tax, FICA, or FUTA.
- *Supplemental Unemployment Benefits.* Costs paid to a welfare fund that provides supplemental unemployment benefits for employees are deductible if the costs are ordinarily and necessary business expenses.
- *Prepaid Legal Expenses.* The exclusion from employee's income for employer-provided group legal service plans is not allowed to the extent that the value of the insurance against legal costs exceeds $70 per year.
- *Compensation for Injuries.* For amounts not compensated for by insurance, you can deduct amounts paid to employees for injuries.
- *Cafeteria Plans.* An employee is not treated as having received cash or a taxable benefit for participation in a cafeteria plan where employees are allowed to choose among two or more benefits consisting of cash and qualified benefits.
- *Fringe Benefits.* You must include in your employee's income the value of fringe benefits you provide for their performing services for you, unless the benefits are specifically excluded from income by law or are paid for by the employee. This includes the following employer-provided items: an automobile, a flight on an employer-provided aircraft, a free or discounted commercial airline flight, a vacation, a discount on property or services, a membership in a country or social club, a ticket to an entertainment or sporting event.
- *Employee Retirement Benefit Plans.* A retirement plan can be funded entirely by the employer, by the employee, or by a mix of both. Payments and deductions become rather complex, requiring the advice and guidance of a pension specialist.

- *Rental Expenses.* In general, you can deduct the cost of rent and associated taxes on property or facilities used in your trade or business, but only if you will not receive equity in or title to the property.
- *Lease Acquisition Cost.* The cost of acquiring a lease must be amortized over the term of the lease.
- *Leasehold Improvements.* The costs of improvements to leased property, such as adding buildings or other permanent improvements, must be depreciated using the modified accelerated cost recovery system (MACRS).
- *Interest Expenses.* Generally, you may pay or accrue the amounts you pay for the use of borrowed money in the tax year on a debt related to your trade or business.
- *Real Estate Taxes.* Ordinarily you can deduct real estate (real property) taxes on property you own, unless you elect to capitalize tax expenses as part of the cost of the property.
- *State and Local Income Taxes.* State income taxes and state tax on gross income (in contrast to net income) directly attributable to a trade or business are deductible as business expenses.
- *Employment Taxes.* As an employer, you are responsible for withholding and paying certain taxes in connection with salaries, wages, tips, certain fringe benefits, and other compensation for your employees, including FICA and FUTA. As an employer, you should deduct the gross amount you pay the employee, including taxes withheld.
- *Personal Property Tax.* You can deduct any tax imposed by a state or local government on personal property used in your trade or business.
- *Sales Tax.* If you acquire depreciable property for use in your business and pay a sales tax, the tax is added to the basis of the property and treated as part of the property's cost for depreciation purposes.
- *Business Insurance.* You can deduct the cost of insurance for your business or profession as a business expense if the insurance is an ordinary and necessary expense in carrying on your trade or business.
- *Medical Health Insurance.* You can deduct contributions you make to provide coverage under a health or accident plan for your employees, unless it provides different benefits to employees with end-stage venereal diseases.
- *Business Bad Debts.* You may generally deduct the amount of a bad debt, that is money due you which you cannot collect, in the year that the debt becomes worthless.
- *Mileage Deductions.* The standard mileage deduction rate is 26 cents a mile for all business miles put onto a car or truck. No longer is there a 15,000 mile annual limit to this deduction.

Deduct or Capitalize?

With some business expenses, you can choose whether to deduct or capitalize. If you choose deduction, you recover it in full immediately. If you capitalize, you recover through depreciation, amortization, or depletion. Included are:

- Certain carrying charges on property.
- Reasonable research and experimental costs.
- Intangible drilling and development costs for oil, gas, and geothermal wells.
- Exploration costs for new mineral deposits.
- Mine development costs for new mineral deposits.
- Costs to increase the circulation of a newspaper or other periodical.
- Costs of making public transportation vehicles, buildings, or other facilities more accessible.

Amortization

You may be able to deduct each year as amortization a part of certain capital expenses. Amortization recovers expenses similar to straight-line depreciation.

Business start-up costs (those for setting up an active trade or business, or investigating the possibility of creating or acquiring an active trade or business) can, under specified conditions, be amortized. Organizational costs directly connected with the creation of the corporation also may, under specified conditions, be amortized.

FILLING IN THE CORPORATE TAX RETURN

Following are sample returns with explanations prepared by the IRS and appearing in IRS Publication 542.

Sample Form 1120-A Return

The following instructions and sample fill-in of Form 1120-A are derived from IRS Publication 542.

Rose Flower Shop, Inc., is the corporation for which the sample return is filled out. Rose Flower Shop is engaged in the business of selling fresh cut flowers and plants. It uses an accrual method of accounting and files its returns on the calendar year.

A corporation may file Form 1120-A if it has gross receipts under $500,000, total income under $500,000, total assets under $500,000, and meets certain other requirements. Since Rose Flower Shop met all these requirements for 1990, it filed the simpler Form 1120-A.

Page 1

If possible when you prepare your return, you should use the pre-addressed label sent to you by the IRS. The pre-addressed label is designed to expedite processing and prevent errors. If you do not have a corporation tax form with a pre-addressed label, enter your corporation's name, street address, city, state, and ZIP code in the appropriate spaces on the first page. After entering the identifying information called for at the top of the page, Rose Flower Shop proceeds to report its items of income and deductions.

The name and employer identification number of the corporation should also be shown in the top margin of schedules and attachments to Form 1120-A.

All applicable items for income, deductions, and tax listed on page 1 of Form 1120-A should be filled in even though totals must be shown on the printed forms. Do not alter, substitute for, or cross out the line captions on the return forms.

Line 1. Gross sales for the year totaled $248,000, using the accrual basis of accounting. After subtracting $7,500 of returned goods and allowances, a net sales figure of $240,500 is entered on line 1c.

Line 2. Cost of goods sold is deducted on line 2. This figure, $144,000, is computed by using the worksheet (not illustrated) provided in the form instructions.

Line 3. Net sales less cost of goods sold results in gross profit of $96,500.

Line 4 through 10. Other items of income are shown next. During the year, the only other item of income for Rose Flower Shop was taxable interest of $942, shown on line 5.

Line 11. Total income amounts to $97,442.

Line 12. The salary of the company president totals $23,000 and is included on line 12.

Line 13. Other salaries and wages total $24,320 and are deducted on line 13a. This includes only salaries and wages not included on line 12 and not deducted as part of cost of goods sold on line 2. Rose Flower Shop was not entitled to a jobs credit, so $24,320 is also entered on line 13c.

Line 16. Rental expense for Rose Flower Shop's place of business was $6,000 for the year.

Line 17. Deductible taxes totaled $3,320.

Line 18. Interest expense accrued during the year amounted to $1,340. Interest to carry tax-exempt securities is not included. See Publication 535, *Business Expenses,* for a discussion of amounts deductible as interest, when the deduction may be taken, and nondeductible items.

Line 19. During 1990, Rose Flower Shop contributed $1,820 to various charitable organizations. The total of $1,820 is less than the limit for deductible contributions, which is 10% of taxable income figured without regard to the contribution deduction.

Line 22. Other deductions consist of $3,000 in advertising expense, entered on this line. If there had been several expenses included in the total, a supporting schedule would be required.

Line 23. Total deductions amount to $62,800.

Lines 24, 25, and 26. Taxable income, $34,642, is shown on line 24. Since Rose Flower Shop did not have a net operating loss or special deduction, $34,642 is also entered on line 26.

Tax summary. Enter on line 27 the total tax ($5,196) from Part I, line 7, page 2. Payments against the tax are listed on line 28. On the Rose Flower Shop return, the only payment is the four estimated tax payments totaling $6,000. It is entered on line 28b, line 28d, and as a total on line 28h. The resulting overpayment is $804, which Rose Flower Shop chooses to have credited to its 1991 estimated tax. Rose Flower Shop could have had the overpayment refunded if it wanted to.

Signature. Rose Flower Shop's return must be signed manually by the corporate officer authorized to sign it.

Page 2

Part I—Tax Computation. The tax computation schedule in the form instructions is used to figure the tax on line 1. Lines 3, 5, and 6, the other taxes and credits listed on

Part I, do not apply to Rose Flower Shop. The tax of $5,196 is entered on lines 1, 4, and 7.

Additional Information. On page 2, all applicable questions must be answered. The business activity code number, business activity, and product or service information must be provided on lines (1), (2), and (3) of question G. Purchases of $134,014 appear on line (1)(a) of question J. Other costs of $9,466 appear on line (1)(c) of question J. The supporting itemization is not illustrated, but these costs consist basically of costs directly related to the sale of flowers, wreaths, and plants, such as flower pots, vases, stands, boxes, wire strands, and tissue paper.

Part II—Balance Sheets. Comparative balance sheets for the beginning and end of the tax year must be provided in Part II. Entries in Part II should agree with amounts shown elsewhere on the return or included on a worksheet. For example, the figures for beginning and ending inventories must be the same as those appearing on the worksheet in the form instructions for cost of goods sold.

Part III—Reconciliation of Income per Books With Income per Return. All Form 1120-A corporate filers must complete Part III. This is so even though Form 1120 corporate filers are not required to complete Schedule M-1, *Reconciliation of Income per Books With Income per Return,* if their total assets are less than $25,000.

To properly complete Part III, first get additional information from your corporation's books and records. The following profit and loss account appeared in the books of Rose Flower Shop for the calendar year 1990.

Account	*Debit*	*Credit*
Gross sales		$248,000
Sales returns and allowances	$ 7,500	
Cost of goods sold	144,000	
Interest income		942
Compensation of officers	23,000	
Salaries and wages	24,320	
Rents	6,000	
Taxes	3,320	
Interest expense	1,340	
Contributions	1,820	
Advertising	3,000	
Federal income tax accrued	5,196	
Net income per books after tax	29,446	
Total	$248,942	$248,942

Part III starts with the net income per books, after reduction for federal income tax accrued, as shown in the corporation's profit and loss account. It provides for necessary adjustments to reconcile this amount with the taxable income shown on line 24, page 1.

Line 1. This is the net income per books, $29,446, shown in the profit and loss account previously as net income per books after tax.

Line 2. This is the federal income tax accrued for the year of the return, $5,196.

Line 7. The taxable income, $34,642, is shown on line 24, page 1 (*Taxable income before net operating loss deduction and special deductions.*)

Form **1120-A** Department of the Treasury Internal Revenue Service

U.S. Corporation Short-Form Income Tax Return

Instructions are separate. See them to make sure you qualify to file Form 1120-A.
For calendar year 1991 or tax year beginning ...., 1991, ending ...., 19 .....

OMB No. 1545-0890 — **1991**

A Check this box if corp. is a personal service corp. (as defined in Temp. Regs. sec. 1.441-4T—see instructions) ▶ ☐

Use IRS label. Otherwise, please print or type.

Name
10-2134567 DEC91 D91 5995
ROSE FLOWER SHOP, INC.
38 SUPERIOR LANE
FAIR CITY, MD 20715

B Employer identification number
C Date incorporated: 7-1-82
D Total assets (see Specific Instructions): $ 65,987

E Check applicable boxes: (1) ☐ Initial return (2) ☐ Change in address
F Check method of accounting: (1) ☐ Cash (2) ☑ Accrual (3) ☐ Other (specify) . . ▶

Income

Line	Description		Amount
1a	Gross receipts or sales 248,000; b Less returns and allowances 7,500; c Balance ▶	1c	240,500
2	Cost of goods sold (see instructions)	2	144,000
3	Gross profit. Subtract line 2 from line 1c	3	96,500
4	Domestic corporation dividends subject to the 70% deduction	4	
5	Interest	5	942
6	Gross rents	6	
7	Gross royalties	7	
8	Capital gain net income (attach Schedule D (Form 1120))	8	
9	Net gain or (loss) from Form 4797, Part II, line 18 (attach Form 4797)	9	
10	Other income (see instructions)	10	
11	**Total income.** Add lines 3 through 10 ▶	11	97,442

Deductions (See instructions for limitations on deductions.)

Line	Description		Amount
12	Compensation of officers (see instructions)	12	23,000
13a	Salaries and wages 24,320; b Less jobs credit ; c Balance ▶	13c	24,320
14	Repairs	14	
15	Bad debts	15	
16	Rents	16	6,000
17	Taxes	17	3,320
18	Interest	18	1,340
19	Contributions (see instructions for 10% limitation)	19	1,820
20	Depreciation (attach Form 4562) — 20		
21	Less depreciation claimed elsewhere on return — 21a	21b	
22	Other deductions (attach schedule) (ADVERTISING)	22	3,000
23	**Total deductions.** Add lines 12 through 22 ▶	23	62,800
24	Taxable income before net operating loss deduction and special deductions. Subtract line 23 from line 11	24	34,642
25	Less: a Net operating loss deduction (see instructions) — 25a; b Special deductions (see instructions) — 25b	25c	

Tax and Payments

Line	Description		Amount
26	**Taxable income.** Subtract line 25c from line 24	26	34,642
27	**Total tax** (from page 2, Part I, line 7)	27	5,146
28	**Payments:**		
a	1990 overpayment credited to 1991 — 28a		
b	1991 estimated tax payments — 28b 6,000		
c	Less 1991 refund applied for on Form 4466 — 28c ( ) Bal ▶ 28d 6,000		
e	Tax deposited with Form 7004 — 28e		
f	Credit from regulated investment companies (attach Form 2439) — 28f		
g	Credit for Federal tax on fuels (attach Form 4136). See instructions — 28g		
h	**Total payments.** Add lines 28d through 28g	28h	6,000
29	**Estimated tax penalty** (see page 4 of instructions). Check if Form 2220 is attached ▶ ☐	29	
30	**Tax due.** If the total of lines 27 and 29 is larger than line 28h, enter amount owed	30	
31	**Overpayment.** If line 28h is larger than the total of lines 27 and 29, enter amount overpaid	31	804
32	Enter amount of line 31 you want: Credited to 1992 estimated tax ▶ 804 Refunded ▶	32	

Please Sign Here

Under penalties of perjury, I declare that I have examined this return, including accompanying schedules and statements, and to the best of my knowledge and belief, it is true, correct, and complete. Declaration of preparer (other than taxpayer) is based on all information of which preparer has any knowledge.

George Rose — Signature of officer | 2-15-92 — Date | President — Title

Paid Preparer's Use Only

Preparer's signature | Date | Check if self-employed ▶ ☐ | Preparer's social security number
Firm's name (or yours if self-employed) and address | E.I. No. ▶ | ZIP code ▶

For Paperwork Reduction Act Notice, see page 1 of the instructions. Cat. No. 11456E Form **1120-A** (1991)

Form 1120-A (1991) Page 2

Part I Tax Computation

1	Income tax (see instructions to figure the tax). Check this box if the corp. is a qualified personal service corp. (see instructions) ▶ ☐	1	5,196
2a	General business credit. Check if from: ☐ Form 3800 ☐ Form 3468 ☐ Form 5884 ☐ Form 6478 ☐ Form 6765 ☐ Form 8586 ☐ Form 8830 ☐ Form 8826 — 2a		
b	Credit for prior year minimum tax (attach Form 8827) — 2b		
3	Total credits. Add lines 2a and 2b	3	
4	Subtract line 3 from line 1	4	5,196
5	Recapture taxes. Check if from: ☐ Form 4255 ☐ Form 8611	5	
6	Alternative minimum tax (attach Form 4623). See instructions	6	
7	Total tax. Add lines 4 through 6. Enter here and on line 27, page 1	7	5,196

Part II Other Information (See page 15 of the instructions.)

1 Refer to the list in the instructions and state the principal:
a Business activity code no. ▶ 5995
b Business activity ▶ Flower Shop
c Product or service ▶ Flowers

2 Did any individual, partnership, estate, or trust at the end of the tax year own, directly or indirectly, 50% or more of the corporation's voting stock? (For rules of attribution, see section 267(c).) ☑ Yes ☐ No

If "Yes," attach schedule showing name, address, and identifying number. (Schedule not illustrated)

3 Enter the amount of tax-exempt interest received or accrued during the tax year ▶ $ -0-

4 Enter amount of cash distributions and the book value of property (other than cash) distributions made in this tax year ▶ $ -0-

5a If an amount is entered on line 2, page 1, see the worksheet on page 11 for amounts to enter below:
(1) Purchases (see instructions) 134,034
(2) Additional sec. 263A costs (see instructions—attach schedule)
(3) Other costs (attach schedule) 9,466

b Do the rules of section 263A (for property produced or acquired for resale) apply to the corporation? ☐ Yes ☑ No

6 At any time during the tax year, did the corporation have an interest in or a signature or other authority over a financial account in a foreign country (such as a bank account, securities account, or other financial account)? (See page 15 of the instructions for filing requirements for Form TD F 90-22.1.) ☐ Yes ☑ No

If "Yes," enter the name of the foreign country ▶

Part III Balance Sheets

		(a) Beginning of tax year	(b) End of tax year
Assets	1 Cash	20,540	18,498
	2a Trade notes and accounts receivable		
	b Less allowance for bad debts	( )	( )
	3 Inventories	2,530	2,010
	4 U.S. government obligations	13,807	45,479
	5 Tax-exempt securities (see instructions)		
	6 Other current assets (attach schedule)		
	7 Loans to stockholders		
	8 Mortgage and real estate loans		
	9a Depreciable, depletable, and intangible assets		
	b Less accumulated depreciation, depletion, and amortization	( )	( )
	10 Land (net of any amortization)		
	11 Other assets (attach schedule)		
	12 Total assets	36,877	65,987
Liabilities and Stockholders' Equity	13 Accounts payable	6,415	6,079
	14 Other current liabilities (attach schedule)		
	15 Loans from stockholders		
	16 Mortgages, notes, bonds payable		
	17 Other liabilities (attach schedule)		
	18 Capital stock (preferred and common stock)	20,000	20,000
	19 Paid-in or capital surplus		
	20 Retained earnings	10,462	39,908
	21 Less cost of treasury stock	( )	( )
	22 Total liabilities and stockholders' equity	36,877	65,987

Part IV Reconciliation of Income per Books With Income per Return (Must be completed by all filers.)

1 Net income per books	29,446	6 Income recorded on books this year not included on this return (itemize)	
2 Federal income tax	5,196	7 Deductions on this return not charged against book income this year (itemize)	
3 Excess of capital losses over capital gains			
4 Income subject to tax not recorded on books this year (itemize)			
5 Expenses recorded on books this year not deducted on this return (itemize)		8 Income (line 24, page 1). Enter the sum of lines 1 through 5 less the sum of lines 6 and 7	34,642

Sample Form 1120 Return

The following instructions and sample fill-in of Form 1120 are derived from IRS Publication 542.

Tentex Toys, Inc. is the corporation for which the sample return is filled out. Tentex is engaged in the business of manufacturing and selling children's toys and games. Is uses an accrual method of accounting and files its returns on the calendar year.

Page 1

When you prepare your return use the pre-addressed label sent to you by the IRS. The pre-addressed label is designed to expedite processing and prevent errors. If you do not have a pre-addressed label, enter your corporation's name, street address, city, state, and ZIP code in the appropriate spaces on the first page. After putting the pre-addressed label at the top of the page, Tentex proceeds to report its income and deductions.

The name and employer identification number of the corporation should also be shown in the top margin of schedules and attachments to Form 1120.

All applicable items for income, deductions, tax, and payments listed on page 1 should be filled in. Do not alter, substitute for, or cross out the line captions on the return forms.

Line 1. Gross sales, line 1a, for the year totaled $2,010,000, using the accrual basis of accounting. After subtracting returned goods and allowances of $20,000, net sales of $1,990,000 is entered on line 1c.

Line 2. Cost of goods sold is deducted on line 2. This figure, $1,520,000, is the total brought over from Schedule A (line 7) on page 2.

Line 3. Net sales less cost of goods sold results in gross profit of $470,000.

Lines 4 through 10. Other items of income are shown next. During the year, Tentex received $10,000 of dividends from domestic corporations, $5,000 of tax-exempt interest from state bonds, and $4,000 of taxable interest. It also received $1,500 interest on its business accounts receivable. The gross amount of dividends is entered on line 4 (note that the dividends-received deduction is taken on line 29b). Total taxable interest of $5,500 is shown on line 5. The tax-exempt interest is not included in income.

Line 11. Total income is $485,500.

Line 12. The salaries of the company president, vice president, and secretary-treasurer, listed on Schedule E, total $70,000 and are included on line 12. Schedule E is completed because total receipts (line 1a plus lines 4 through 10 of page 1) are $500,000 or more.

Line 13. Other salaries and wages total $44,000 and are entered on line 13a. This includes only salaries and wages not included on line 12 and not deducted as part of cost of goods sold on line 3, Schedule A on page 2. For a manufacturing company such as Tentex, this amount represents nonmanufacturing salaries and wages, such as office salaries. See Chapter 2 of Publication 535 for a discussion of salaries and wages. Tentex is eligible for a $6,000 targeted jobs credit, which is figured on Form 5884 (not illustrated). The deduction for salaries and wages is reduced on line 13b by the allowable $6,000 credit. The balance, $38,000, is entered on line 13c.

Line 14. Repairs include only payments for items that do not add to the value of the assets repaired or substantially increase their useful lives. Repairs total $800. See Chapter 13 of Publication 535 for information on repairs, improvements, and replacements.

Line 15. Tentex uses the specific charge-off method of accounting for bad debts. Actual accounts written off during the year total $1,600. See Chapter 12 of Publication 535 for information on bad debt deductions.

Line 16. Rent for Tentex's office facilities was $9,200 for the year.

Line 17. Deductible taxes are $15,000.

Line 18. Interest expense accrued during the year amounted to $27,200. This included interest both on debts for business operations and debts to carry investments. Interest to carry tax-exempt securities is not included. See Chapter 6 of Publication 535 for a discussion of amounts deductible as interest.

Line 19. During 1991, Tentex contributed $11,400 to the United Community Fund and $12,600 to the State University scholarship fund. The total, $24,000, is more than the limit for deductible contributions, which is 10% of taxable income figured without the contribution deduction and special deduction entered on line 29b. The amount allowable under the limit is $23,150, and this is entered on line 19. The excess, $850, not deductible this year, may be carried over as explained earlier under *Charitable Contributions*. Also, during 1991, Tentex made nondeductible contributions of $500.

Lines 20 and 21. Depreciation of $17,600 is brought forward from Form 4562 (not illustrated) and entered on line 20. This amount is reduced by the depreciation claimed on Schedule A ($12,400) and entered on line 21a. The balance ($5,200) is deducted on line 21b since it is the depreciation on the assets used in the indirect operations of the business.

Line 22. Depletion is entered on line 22. This item did not affect Tentex. See Chapter 11 of Publication 535.

Line 23. Advertising expense is $8,700.

Lines 24 and 25. Profit-sharing, stock bonus, pension, and annuity plans are discussed in Chapter 4 of Publication 535. Tentex does not have any of these plans.

Line 26. Other ordinary and necessary business deductions totaled $78,300. These included miscellaneous office expenses, sales commissions, legal fees, etc. A schedule itemizing these expenses must be attached to the return, even though it is not shown in this example.

Line 27. Total of lines 12 through 26 is $277,150.

Lines 28, 29, and 30. Taxable income, $208,350, is shown on line 28. Since Tentex did not have a net operating loss, its only entry on line 29 is the special dividends-received deduction of $8,000 brought forward from Schedule C, page 2. This is entered on lines 29b and 29c. Taxable income on line 30 is $200,350.

Tax summary. Enter on line 31 the total tax ($55,387) form Schedule J. Payments against the tax are listed on line 32. On the Tentex return, the only credit is the four estimated tax payments totaling $69,117. It is entered on lines 32b, 32d, and 32h. The resulting overpayment is $13,730, which Tentex chooses to have credited to its 1992 estimated tax. Tentex could have the overpayment refunded.

Signature. Tentex's return must be signed manually by a corporate officer authorized to sign it.

Page 2

Schedule A. Use Schedule A to report your cost of goods sold. Basically, this figure is beginning inventory, plus merchandise bought or produced during the year, less ending inventory. Because it is a manufacturer, Tentex must account for its costs of manufacturing as part of cost of goods sold. Goods on hand at the beginning of the year were valued at $126,000, using the lower of cost or market method of inventory valuation.

Cost of good manufactured during the year is added to beginning inventory. This cost is made up of three items: direct materials, direct labor, and overhead. Materials cost of $1,127,100 is listed on line 2; this includes subcontracted parts as well as raw materials.

Salaries and wages of $402,000 are entered on line 3. This amount includes wages paid to production-line workers and also the part of supervisory salaries attributable to actual production of goods. It also includes 30% of the salaries paid to officers. Do not deduct payments already deducted on line 12 or 13 of page 1.

The $40,000 on line 4a is for indirect general administration costs. Other costs of $123,300 appear on line 4b. The supporting itemization is not illustrated, but these costs consist basically of factory overhead such as electricity, fuel, water, small tools, and depreciation on production-line machinery. Note that this depreciation ($12,400) represents depreciation on the assets used in the direct operations of the business.

Line 8. Check all applicable boxes.

Schedule C. Dividend income is $10,000, all of which qualified for the 80% dividends-received deduction, line 2, because Tentex is a 20%-or-more owner. Total dividends are shown both here and on line 4 of page 1. The total dividends-received deduction is figured here and entered on line 29b of page 1.

Schedule E. Complete this schedule only if your total receipts (line 1a plus lines 4 through 10 of page 1) are $500,000 or more. (Tentex meets this requirement.) Since Tentex has only three corporate officers, these are the only entries on the schedule. Only compensation for services rendered is included here. Do not include dividends on stock held by the corporate officers.

Page 3

Schedule J. Use Schedule J to figure the corporation's tax. Applying the rates to Tentex's taxable income of $200,350 results in an income tax figure of $61,387. This figure is decreased by the jobs credit of $6,000, resulting in a total tax of $55,387.

The jobs credit is figured by multiplying $15,000 of wages paid to five qualified summer youth clerical employees (who were certified as members of a targeted group) in their first year of employment by the 40% rate. Each member earned $3,000 in salary in 1991. Form 5884 (not illustrated) is filed with Tentex's return to support this credit.

Other taxes and credits listed on Schedule J do not apply to Tentex for 1991.

Schedule K. Answer all applicable questions.

Page 4

Schedule L. Provide comparative balance sheets for the beginning and end of the tax year. Entries on this page should agree with amounts shown elsewhere on the return. For example, the figures for beginning and ending inventories must be the same as those appearing on Schedule A, page 2. Note that the appropriated retained earnings of Tentex increased from $30,000 to $40,000 during the year, due to the setting aside of $10,000 as a reserve for contingencies. This amount was taken out of unappropriated retained earnings, as shown on Schedule M-2.

Schedules M-1 and M-2 are completed if the total assets (line 15, column (d), Schedule L) are $25,000 or more. To properly complete these schedules, you must first get additional information from your corporation's books and records. The following profit and loss account appeared in the books of Tentex for the calendar year 1991.

Account		*Debit*	*Credit*
Gross sales			$2,010,000
Sales returns and allowances		$ 20,000	
Cost of goods sold		1,520,000	
Dividends received			10,000
Interest income (on state bonds)	$ 5,000		
(other-taxable)	5,500		10,500
Proceeds of life insurance			9,500
Premiums on life insurance		9,500	
Compensation of officers		70,000	
Salaries and wages-indirect		44,000	
Repairs		800	
Bad debts		1,600	
Rental expense		9,200	
Taxes		15,000	
Interest expense			
(on loan to buy			
tax-exempt bonds)	$ 850		
(other)	27,200	28,050	
Contributions			
(deductible)	$24,000		
(nondeductible)	500	24,500	
Depreciation-indirect		3,580	
Advertising		8,700	
Other expenses of operation		78,300	
Loss on securities		3,600	
Federal income tax accrued		55,387	
Net income per books after tax		147,783	
Total		$2,040,000	$2,040,000

Retained earnings were analyzed and the following appeared in this account in the books of the corporation:

Item	*Debit*	*Credit*
Balance, January 1, 1991		$238,000
Net profit (before federal income tax)		203,170
Reserve for contingencies	$ 10,000	
Income tax accrued for 1991	55,387	
Dividends paid during 1991	65,000	
Refund of 1989 income tax		18,000
Balance, December 31, 1991	328,783	
Total	$459,170	$459,170

Schedule M-1. Schedule M-1 starts with the net income per books, after allowance of federal income tax accrued, as shown in the corporation's profit and loss account. It provides for necessary adjustments to reconcile this amount with the taxable income shown on line 28, page 1.

Line 1. This is the net income per books, $147,783, shown in the profit and loss account previously as net income per books after tax.

Line 2. This is the federal income tax accrued for the year of the return, $55,387.

Line 3. This is for the capital losses that exceed capital gains. The net loss on securities, $3,600, is entered.

Line 4. This would show all income and credits included in income subject to tax that are not recorded on the books for this year. This can happen if assets are valued in the corporate books at an amount greater than that used for tax purposes. When a sale of such assets is made, the gain included in taxable income is greater than that recorded on the books, and the difference is shown here.

Line 5. This is for expenses recorded on the corporation's books that may not be deducted. Besides the $850 listed on line 5b as contributions that were over the 10% limit, the remaining nondeductible expenses are shown in an itemized statement (not illustrated) attached to the return that would include the following:

Premiums paid on term life insurance on corporate officers	$ 9,500
Interest paid to purchase tax-exempt securities	850
Nondeductible contributions	500
Reduction of salaries by jobs credit	6,000
Total	$16,850

Line 6. This is the total of lines 1 through 5.

Line 7. This shows nontaxable income recorded on the corporation's books during the year that is not on the return. This total, $14,500, includes insurance proceeds of $9,500 and interest on state bonds of $5,000.

Line 8. This includes all deductions claimed for tax purposes that are not recorded in the corporation's books. Tentex enters $1,620 on line 8a. This is the difference between depreciation claimed on the tax return and the corporation's books. If the corporation had other deductions to itemize on this line and there was not enough space on the line, it would have to attach a statement to the return listing them.

Line 9. This shows the total of lines 7 and 8, or $16,120.

Line 10. The difference, $208,350, between lines 6 and 9 must agree with line 28, page 1.

Schedule M-2. Schedule M-2 analyzes the unappropriated retained earnings as shown in Schedule L, the corporation's balance sheets.

Line 1. This is from line 25 of Schedule L for the beginning of the tax year. Tentex enters $238,000.

Line 2. This is the net income per books (after federal income tax), $147,783.

Line 3. This shows all other increases to retained earnings. The refund of 1989 income tax, $18,000, is entered.

Line 4. This is the total of lines 1, 2, and 3.

Line 5. This includes all distributions to shareholders charged to retained earnings during the tax year. The dividends paid, $65,000, are entered.

Line 6. This shows any decreases (other than those on Line 5) in unappropriated retained earnings. These decreases are not deductible on the tax return at the time of the appropriation, but a deduction may be allowable at a later date. A common example is amounts set aside for contingencies. A customer was injured on company property during 1991 and the company retained an attorney. A contingent liability of $10,000 was set up for the customer's claim. If this claim is settled during 1992 for $5,000 and the attorney's fee is $2,500, the retained earnings (appropriated) would be charged $7,500. The $7,500 would be deducted in arriving at taxable income for 1992. Another common example of items entered on this line is the payment of prior year's federal tax. A schedule must be attached to the return listing all items taken into account to arrive at the amount shown on this line.

Line 7. This is the total of lines 5 and 6.

Line 8. This shows the retained earnings of the corporation at the end of the tax year for which the return is made. This figure is determined by subtracting the total on line 7 from the total on line 4. The figure must agree with the amount shown on Schedule L for the end of the year for which the return is made. As shown, $328,783 is entered on Schedule L.

Form **1120** Department of the Treasury Internal Revenue Service

U.S. Corporation Income Tax Return

For calendar year 1991 or tax year beginning ...., 1991, ending ...., 19 ...

▶ **Instructions are separate. See page 1 for Paperwork Reduction Act Notice.**

OMB No. 1545-0123 **1991**

A Check if a—
(1) Consolidated return (attach Form 851) ☐
(2) Personal holding co. (attach Sch. PH) ☐
(3) Personal service corp. (as defined in Temp. Regs. sec. 1.441-4T—see instructions) ☐

Use IRS label. Otherwise, please print or type.

10-0395674 DEC91 071 3998
TENTEX TOYS, INC.
36 DIVISION STREET
ANYTOWN, IL 60930

B Employer identification number

C Date incorporated: 3-1-72

D Total assets (see Specific Instructions): $ 879,417

E Check applicable boxes: (1) ☐ Initial return (2) ☐ Final return (3) ☐ Change in address

Income

Line	Description		Amount
1a	Gross receipts or sales 2,010,000 b Less returns and allowances 20,000 c Bal ▶	1c	1,990,000
2	Cost of goods sold (Schedule A, line 7)	2	1,520,000
3	Gross profit. Subtract line 2 from line 1c	3	470,000
4	Dividends (Schedule C, line 19)	4	10,000
5	Interest	5	5,500
6	Gross rents	6	
7	Gross royalties	7	
8	Capital gain net income (attach Schedule D (Form 1120))	8	
9	Net gain or (loss) from Form 4797, Part II, line 18 (attach Form 4797)	9	
10	Other income (see instructions—attach schedule)	10	
11	**Total income.** Add lines 3 through 10 ▶	11	485,500

Deductions (See instructions for limitations on deductions.)

Line	Description		Amount
12	Compensation of officers (Schedule E, line 4)	12	70,000
13a	Salaries and wages 44,000 b Less jobs credit 6,000 c Balance ▶	13c	38,000
14	Repairs	14	800
15	Bad debts	15	1,600
16	Rents	16	9,200
17	Taxes	17	15,000
18	Interest	18	27,200
19	Contributions (**see instructions for 10% limitation**)	19	23,150
20	Depreciation (attach Form 4562) — 20: 17,600		
21	Less depreciation claimed on Schedule A and elsewhere on return — 21a: 12,400	21b	5,200
22	Depletion	22	
23	Advertising	23	8,700
24	Pension, profit-sharing, etc., plans	24	
25	Employee benefit programs	25	
26	Other deductions (attach schedule)	26	78,300
27	**Total deductions.** Add lines 12 through 26 ▶	27	277,150
28	Taxable income before net operating loss deduction and special deductions. Subtract line 27 from line 11	28	208,350
29	**Less:** a Net operating loss deduction (see instructions) — 29a		
	b Special deductions (Schedule C, line 20) — 29b: 8,000	29c	8,000

Tax and Payments

Line	Description		Amount
30	**Taxable income.** Subtract line 29c from line 28	30	200,350
31	**Total tax** (Schedule J, line 10)	31	55,387
32	**Payments:** a 1990 overpayment credited to 1991 — 32a		
b	1991 estimated tax payments — 32b: 69,117		
c	Less 1991 refund applied for on Form 4466 — 32c ( ) d Bal ▶ 32d: 69,117		
e	Tax deposited with Form 7004 — 32e		
f	Credit from regulated investment companies (attach Form 2439) — 32f		
g	Credit for Federal tax on fuels (attach Form 4136). See instructions — 32g	32h	69,117
33	Estimated tax penalty (see page 4 of instructions). Check if Form 2220 is attached ▶ ☐	33	
34	**Tax due.** If the total of lines 31 and 33 is larger than line 32h, enter amount owed	34	
35	**Overpayment.** If line 35h is larger than the total of lines 31 and 33, enter amount overpaid	35	13,730
36	Enter amount of line 35 you want: **Credited to 1992 estimated tax** ▶ 13,730 Refunded ▶	36	

Please Sign Here

Under penalties of perjury, I declare that I have examined this return, including accompanying schedules and statements, and to the best of my knowledge and belief, it is true, correct, and complete. Declaration of preparer (other than taxpayer) is based on all information of which preparer has any knowledge.

▶ James Q Barclay (Signature of officer) | 3-7-92 (Date) | ▶ President (Title)

Paid Preparer's Use Only

Preparer's signature ▶ | Date | Check if self-employed ☐ | Preparer's social security number

Firm's name (or yours if self-employed) and address ▶ | E.I. No. ▶ | ZIP code ▶

Cat. No. 11450Q

Form 1120 (1991) Page 2

Schedule A — Cost of Goods Sold (See instructions.)

1	Inventory at beginning of year	1	126,000
2	Purchases	2	1,127,100
3	Cost of labor	3	402,000
4a	Additional section 263A costs (see instructions—attach schedule)	4a	40,000
b	Other costs (attach schedule)	4b	123,300
5	**Total.** Add lines 1 through 4b	5	1,818,400
6	Inventory at end of year	6	298,400
7	**Cost of goods sold.** Subtract line 6 from line 5. Enter here and on line 2, page 1	7	1,520,000

8a Check all methods used for valuing closing inventory:
(i) ☐ Cost (ii) ☑ Lower of cost or market as described in Regulations section 1.471-4 (see instructions)
(iii) ☐ Writedown of "subnormal" goods as described in Regulations section 1.471-2(c) (see instructions)
(iv) ☐ Other (Specify method used and attach explanation.) ▶

b Check if the LIFO inventory method was adopted this tax year for any goods (if checked, attach Form 970) ▶ ☐

c If the LIFO inventory method was used for this tax year, enter percentage (or amounts) of closing inventory computed under LIFO | 8c |

d Do the rules of section 263A (for property produced or acquired for resale) apply to the corporation? ☑ Yes ☐ No

e Was there any change in determining quantities, cost, or valuations between opening and closing inventory? If "Yes," attach explanation ☐ Yes ☑ No

Schedule C — Dividends and Special Deductions (See instructions.)

		(a) Dividends received	(b) %	(c) Special deductions: (a) × (b)
1	Dividends from less-than-20%-owned domestic corporations that are subject to the 70% deduction (other than debt-financed stock)		70	
2	Dividends from 20%-or-more-owned domestic corporations that are subject to the 80% deduction (other than debt-financed stock)	10,000	80	8,000
3	Dividends on debt-financed stock of domestic and foreign corporations (section 246A)		see instructions	
4	Dividends on certain preferred stock of less-than-20%-owned public utilities		41.176	
5	Dividends on certain preferred stock of 20%-or-more-owned public utilities		47.059	
6	Dividends from less-than-20%-owned foreign corporations and certain FSCs that are subject to the 70% deduction		70	
7	Dividends from 20%-or-more-owned foreign corporations and certain FSCs that are subject to the 80% deduction		80	
8	Dividends from wholly owned foreign subsidiaries subject to the 100% deduction (section 245(b))		100	
9	**Total.** Add lines 1 through 8. See instructions for limitation			8,000
10	Dividends from domestic corporations received by a small business investment company operating under the Small Business Investment Act of 1958		100	
11	Dividends from certain FSCs that are subject to the 100% deduction (section 245(c)(1))		100	
12	Dividends from affiliated group members subject to the 100% deduction (section 243(a)(3))		100	
13	Other dividends from foreign corporations not included on lines 3, 6, 7, 8, or 11			
14	Income from controlled foreign corporations under subpart F (attach Forms 5471)			
15	Foreign dividend gross-up (section 78)			
16	IC-DISC and former DISC dividends not included on lines 1, 2, or 3 (section 246(d))			
17	Other dividends			
18	Deduction for dividends paid on certain preferred stock of public utilities (see instructions)			
19	**Total dividends.** Add lines 1 through 17. Enter here and on line 4, page 1 ▶	10,000		
20	**Total deductions.** Add lines 9, 10, 11, 12, and 18. Enter here and on line 29b, page 1 ▶			8,000

Schedule E — Compensation of Officers (See instructions for line 12, page 1.)

Complete Schedule E only if total receipts (line 1a plus lines 4 through 10 of page 1, Form 1120) are $500,000 or more.

	(a) Name of officer	(b) Social security number	(c) Percent of time devoted to business	Percent of corporation stock owned: (d) Common	(e) Preferred	(f) Amount of compensation
1	James O. Barclay	581-00-0936	100 %	45 %	%	55,000
			%	%	%	
	George M. Collins	447-00-2604	100 %	15 %	%	31,000
			%	%	%	
	Samuel Adams	401-00-2611	50 %	2 %	%	14,000
2	Total compensation of officers					100,000
3	**Less:** Compensation of officers claimed on Schedule A and elsewhere on return					(30,000)
4	Compensation of officers deducted on line 12, page 1					70,000

Form 1120 (1991) Page 3

Schedule J Tax Computation

1	Check if you are a member of a controlled group (see sections 1561 and 1563) ▶ ☐		
2	If the box on line 1 is checked:		
a	Enter your share of the $50,000 and $25,000 taxable income bracket amounts (in that order): (i) $ (ii) $		
b	Enter your share of the additional 5% tax (not to exceed $11,750) ▶ $		
3	Income tax (see instructions to figure the tax). Check this box if the corporation is a qualified personal service corporation (see instructions on page 13) ▶ ☐	3	61,387
4a	Foreign tax credit (attach Form 1118)	4a	
b	Possessions tax credit (attach Form 5735)	4b	
c	Orphan drug credit (attach Form 6765)	4c	
d	Credit for fuel produced from a nonconventional source (see instructions)	4d	
e	General business credit. Enter here and check which forms are attached: ☐ Form 3800 ☐ Form 3468 ☑ Form 5884 ☐ Form 6478 ☐ Form 6765 ☐ Form 8586 ☐ Form 8830 ☐ Form 8826	4e	6,000
f	Credit for prior year minimum tax (attach Form 8827)	4f	
5	**Total.** Add lines 4a through 4f	5	6,000
6	Subtract line 5 from line 3	6	55,387
7	Personal holding company tax (attach Schedule PH (Form 1120))	7	
8	Recapture taxes. Check if from: ☐ Form 4255 ☐ Form 8611	8	
9a	Alternative minimum tax (attach Form 4626). See instructions	9a	
b	Environmental tax (attach Form 4626)	9b	
10	**Total tax.** Add lines 6 through 9b. Enter here and on line 31, page 1	10	55,387

Schedule K Other Information (See page 15 of the instructions.)

		Yes	No
1	Check method of accounting: a ☐ Cash b ☑ Accrual c ☐ Other (specify) ▶		
2	Refer to the list in the instructions and state the principal:		
a	Business activity code no. ▶ 3998		
b	Business activity ▶ Manufacturing		
c	Product or service ▶ Toys		
3	Did the corporation at the end of the tax year own, directly or indirectly, 50% or more of the voting stock of a domestic corporation? (For rules of attribution, see section 267(c).)		✓
	If "Yes," attach a schedule showing: (a) name, address, and identifying number; (b) percentage owned; and (c) taxable income or (loss) before NOL and special deductions of such corporation for the tax year ending with or within your tax year.		
4	Did any individual, partnership, corporation, estate, or trust at the end of the tax year own, directly or indirectly, 50% or more of the corporation's voting stock? (For rules of attribution, see section 267(c).) If "Yes," complete **a** and **b**		✓
a	Attach a schedule showing name, address, and identifying number.		
b	Enter percentage owned ▶		
5	Did one foreign person (see instructions for definition) at any time during the tax year own at least 25% of:		
a	The total voting power of all classes of stock of the corporation entitled to vote, or		
b	The total value of all classes of stock of the corporation?		✓
	If "Yes," the corporation may have to file Form 5472. If "Yes," enter owner's country(ies) ▶ Enter number of Forms 5472 attached ▶		
6	Was the corporation a U.S. shareholder of any controlled foreign corporation? (See sections 951 and 957.)		✓
	If "Yes," attach Form 5471 for each such corporation. Enter number of Forms 5471 attached ▶		
7	At any time during the tax year, did the corporation have an interest in or a signature or other authority over a financial account in a foreign country (such as a bank account, securities account, or other financial account)? (See page 15 of the instructions for more information, including filing requirements for Form TD F 90-22.1.)		✓
	If "Yes," enter name of foreign country ▶		
8	Was the corporation the grantor of, or transferor to, a foreign trust that existed during the current tax year, whether or not the corporation has any beneficial interest in it?		✓
	If "Yes," the corporation may have to file Forms 3520, 3520-A, or 926.		
9	During this tax year, did the corporation pay dividends (other than stock dividends and distributions in exchange for stock) in excess of the corporation's current and accumulated earnings and profits? (See sections 301 and 316.)		✓
	If "Yes," file Form 5452. If this is a consolidated return, answer here for parent corporation and on **Form 851,** Affiliations Schedule, for each subsidiary.		
10	Check this box if the corporation issued publicly offered debt instruments with original issue discount ▶ ☐ If so, the corporation may have to file Form 8281.		
11	Enter the amount of tax-exempt interest received or accrued during the tax year ▶ $ 5,000		
12	If there were 35 or fewer shareholders at the end of the tax year, enter the number ▶		

Form 1120 (1991) Page 4

Schedule L Balance Sheets

		Beginning of tax year		End of tax year	
	Assets	(a)	(b)	(c)	(d)
1	Cash		14,700		28,331
2a	Trade notes and accounts receivable	98,400		103,700	
b	Less allowance for bad debts	( )	98,400	( )	103,700
3	Inventories		126,000		298,400
4	U.S. government obligations				
5	Tax-exempt securities (see instructions)		100,000		120,000
6	Other current assets (attach schedule)		26,300		17,266
7	Loans to stockholders				
8	Mortgage and real estate loans				
9	Other investments (attach schedule)		100,000		80,000
10a	Buildings and other depreciable assets	272,400		296,700	
b	Less accumulated depreciation	(88,300)	184,100	(104,280)	192,420
11a	Depletable assets				
b	Less accumulated depletion	( )		( )	
12	Land (net of any amortization)		20,000		20,000
13a	Intangible assets (amortizable only)				
b	Less accumulated amortization	( )		( )	
14	Other assets (attach schedule)		14,800		19,300
15	Total assets		684,300		879,417
	Liabilities and Stockholders' Equity				
16	Accounts payable		28,500		34,834
17	Mortgages, notes, bonds payable in less than 1 year		4,300		4,300
18	Other current liabilities (attach schedule)		6,800		7,400
19	Loans from stockholders				
20	Mortgages, notes, bonds payable in 1 year or more		176,700		264,100
21	Other liabilities (attach schedule)				
22	Capital stock: a Preferred stock				
	b Common stock	200,000	200,000	200,000	200,000
23	Paid-in or capital surplus				
24	Retained earnings—Appropriated (attach schedule)		30,000		40,000
25	Retained earnings—Unappropriated		238,000		328,783
26	Less cost of treasury stock		( )		( )
27	Total liabilities and stockholders' equity		684,300		879,417

Schedule M-1 Reconciliation of Income per Books With Income per Return *(This schedule does not have to be completed if the total assets on line 15, column (d), of Schedule L are less than $25,000.)*

1	Net income per books	147,783	7	Income recorded on books this year not included on this return (itemize):	
2	Federal income tax	55,387		a Tax-exempt interest $ 5000	
3	Excess of capital losses over capital gains	3,600		b Insurance Proceeds 9,500	14,500
4	Income subject to tax not recorded on books this year (itemize):		8	Deductions on this return not charged against book income this year (itemize):	
5	Expenses recorded on books this year not deducted on this return (itemize):			a Depreciation $ 1,620	
a	Depreciation $			b Contributions carryover $	
b	Contributions carryover $ 850				
c	Travel and entertainment $ See Itemized statement attached 16,850	17,700			1,620
			9	Add lines 7 and 8	16,120
6	Add lines 1 through 5	224,470	10	Income (line 28, page 1)—line 6 less line 9	208,350

Schedule M-2 Analysis of Unappropriated Retained Earnings per Books (Line 25, Schedule L) *(This schedule does not have to be completed if the total assets on line 15, column (d), of Schedule L are less than $25,000.)*

1	Balance at beginning of year	238,000	5	Distributions: a Cash	65,000
2	Net income per books	147,783		b Stock	
3	Other increases (itemize):			c Property	
	Refund of 1989 Income Tax Due to IRS Examination		6	Other decreases (itemize): Reserve for Contingencies	10,000
		18,000	7	Add lines 5 and 6	75,000
4	Add lines 1, 2, and 3	403,783	8	Balance at end of year (line 4 less line 7)	328,783

SCHEDULE D (Form 1120)

Department of the Treasury
Internal Revenue Service

Capital Gains and Losses

To be filed with Forms 1120, 1120-A, 1120-DF, 1120-IC-DISC, 1120F, 1120-FSC, 1120-H, 1120L, 1120-ND, 1120-PC, 1120-POL, 1120-REIT, 1120-RIC, 990-C, and certain Forms 990-T

OMB No. 1545-0123

1991

Name | **Employer identification number**

Part I **Short-Term Capital Gains and Losses—Assets Held 1 Year or Less**

(a) Kind of property and description (Example, 100 shares of "Z" Co.)	**(b)** Date acquired (mo., day, yr.)	**(c)** Date sold (mo., day, yr.)	**(d)** Gross sales price	**(e)** Cost or other basis, plus expense of sale	**(f)** Gain or (loss) ((d) less (e))
1					

2	Short-term capital gain from installment sales from Form 6252, line 22 or 30	2	
3	Unused capital loss carryover (attach computation)	3	( )
4	Net short-term capital gain or (loss). (Combine lines 1 through 3.)	4	

Part II **Long-Term Capital Gains and Losses—Assets Held More Than 1 Year**

5					

6	Enter gain from Form 4797, line 7 or 9	6	
7	Long-term capital gain from installment sales from Form 6252, line 22 or 30	7	
8	Net long-term capital gain or (loss). (Combine lines 5 through 7.)	8	

Part III **Summary of Parts I and II**

9	Enter excess of net short-term capital gain (line 4) over net long-term capital loss (line 8)	9	
10	Net capital gain. Enter excess of net long-term capital gain (line 8) over net short-term capital loss (line 4)	10	
11	Add lines 9 and 10. Enter here and on Form 1120, line 8, page 1; or the proper line on other returns	11	

Note: *If losses exceed gains, see instructions on capital losses for explanation of capital loss carrybacks.*

Instructions

(Section references are to the Internal Revenue Code.)

Purpose of Schedule

Schedule D is used to report sales and exchanges of capital assets for tax years beginning in 1991 if one of the following forms is being filed: Forms 1120, 1120-A, 1120-DF, 1120-IC-DISC, 1120F, 1120-FSC, 1120-H, 1120L, 1120-ND, 1120-PC, 1120-POL, 1120-REIT, 1120-RIC, 990-C, or certain Forms 990-T.

Sales or exchanges of property other than capital assets are reported on **Form 4797,** Sales of Business Property. A sale or exchange of property includes property used in a trade or business, involuntary conversions (other than casualties or thefts), gain from the disposition of oil, gas, or geothermal property, and the section 291 adjustment to section 1250 gains. See the instructions for Form 4797 for more information.

If property is involuntarily converted because of a casualty or theft, use **Form 4684,** Casualties and Thefts.

Parts I and II

Generally, a corporation must report sales and exchanges, including "like-kind" exchanges, even though there is no gain or loss. No loss is allowed for a wash sale of stock or securities (including contracts or options to acquire or sell stock or securities) or from a transaction between related persons. See sections 1091 and 267 for details and exceptions.

Use Part I to report the sale or exchange of capital assets held 1 year or less. Use Part II to report the sale or exchange of capital assets held more than 1 year.

What Is a Capital Asset?—Each item of property the corporation held (whether or not connected with its trade or business) is a capital asset except:

1. Assets that can be inventoried or property held mainly for sale to customers.

2. Depreciable or real property used in the trade or business.

3. Certain copyrights; literary, musical, or artistic compositions; letters or memorandums; or similar property.

4. Accounts or notes receivable acquired in the ordinary course of trade or business for services rendered or from the sale of property described in 1 above.

5. A U.S. Government publication (including the Congressional Record) received from the Government or any of its agencies in a manner other than buying it at the price offered for public sale, which is held by a taxpayer who received the publication or by a second taxpayer in whose hands the basis of the publication is determined, for purposes of determining gain from a sale or exchange, by referring to its basis in the hands of the first taxpayer.

Exchange of "like-kind" property.—A "like-kind exchange" occurs when the corporation exchanges business or investment property for property of like kind. Report the exchange of like-kind property on Schedule D or Form 4797, whichever applies, even if no gain or loss is recognized. Also, complete and attach to the tax return **Form 8824,** Like-Kind Exchanges, for each exchange.

On Schedule D, write "From Form 8824" for the description of the property, and enter the gain or loss from Form 8824, if any. If an exchange was made with a related party, write "Related Party Like-Kind Exchange" in the top margin of Schedule D.

Capital losses.—Capital losses are allowed only to the extent of capital gains. A net capital loss may be carried back 3 years and forward 5 years as a short-term capital loss. Carry back a capital loss to the extent it does not increase or produce a net operating loss in the tax year to which it is carried. Foreign expropriation capital losses may not be carried back, but may be carried forward 10 years. A net capital loss for a regulated investment company may be carried forward 8 years.

Special Rules for the Treatment of Certain Gains and Losses

Note: *For more information, get* ***Pub. 544,*** *Sales and Other Dispositions of Assets, and* ***Pub. 542,*** *Tax Information on Corporations. See the cited code sections for details.*

- **At-risk limitations (section 465).**—If the corporation sold or exchanged a capital asset used in an activity to which the at-risk rules apply, combine the gain or loss on the sale or exchange with the profit or loss from the activity. If the result is a net loss, complete **Form 6198,** At-Risk Limitations. Report any gain from the capital asset on Schedule D and on Form 6198.
- **Gains and losses from passive activities.**—A closely held or personal service corporation that has a gain or loss which relates to a passive activity (section 469) may be required to complete **Form 8810,** Corporate Passive Activity Loss and Credit Limitations, before completing Schedule D. A Schedule D loss may be limited under the passive activity rules. See Form 8810 for more detailed information.
- **Gain on distributions of appreciated property.**—Generally, gain (but not loss) is recognized on a nonliquidating distribution of appreciated property to the extent that the property's fair market value exceeds its adjusted basis. See section 311 for more information.
- **Gain or loss on distribution of property in complete liquidation.**—Generally, gain or loss is recognized on property distributed in a complete liquidation. Treat the property as if it had been sold at its fair market value. An exception to this rule applies for liquidations of certain subsidiaries. See sections 336 and 337 for more information and other exceptions to the general rules.
- **Gains and losses on section 1256 contracts and straddles.**—Use **Form 6781,** Gains and Losses From Section 1256 Contracts and Straddles, to report these gains and losses.
- **Gain or loss on certain short-term Federal, state, and municipal obligations.**—Such obligations are treated as capital assets in determining gain or loss. On any gain realized, a portion is treated as ordinary income and the balance as a short-term capital gain. See section 1271.
- **Gain from installment sales.**—Use **Form 6252,** Installment Sale Income, to report a gain from the casual sale of real or personal property (other than inventory) if payments will be received in more than one tax year. See the instructions below for how to elect out of the installment method. Also use Form 6252 if a payment is received this year from a sale made in an earlier year on the installment method.

To elect out of the installment method, report the following on a timely filed return (including extensions):

1. Include the full amount of the sale on Schedule D.

2. If the corporation received a note or other obligation and is reporting it at less than face value (including all contingent obligations), state that fact in the margin and give the percentage of valuation.

The installment method may not be used for sales of stock or securities (or certain other property described in the regulations) traded on an established securities market. See section 453(k).

- **Gain or loss on an option to buy or sell property.**—See sections 1032 and 1234 for the rules that apply to a purchaser or grantor of an option.
- **Gain or loss from a short sale of property.**—Report the gain or loss to the extent that the property used to close the short sale is considered a capital asset in the hands of the taxpayer.
- **Gains and losses of foreign corporations from the disposition of investment in United States real property.**—Foreign corporations are required to report gains and losses from the disposition of U.S. real property interests. See section 897 for details.
- **Gains on certain insurance property.**—Form 1120L filers with gains on property held on December 31, 1958, and certain substituted property acquired after 1958 should see section 818(c).
- **Gain or loss from shares purchased in a regulated investment company (RIC).**—In some cases, the load charge (advance charge for sales fees) incurred to purchase shares in a RIC may not be allowed when figuring the basis for gain or loss on the disposition of the shares. See section 852(f) if the shares were disposed of within 90 days of purchase, and the load charge on stock subsequently acquired in that RIC (or another RIC) was reduced because of a reinvestment right.
- **Loss from the sale or exchange of capital assets of an insurance company taxable under section 831.**—Under the provisions of section 834(c)(6), capital losses of a casualty insurance company are deductible to the extent that the assets were sold to meet abnormal insurance losses or to provide for the payment of dividend and similar distributions to policyholders.
- **Loss from securities that are capital assets that become worthless during the year.**—Except for securities held by a bank, treat the loss as a capital loss as of the last day of the tax year. (See section 582 for the rules on the treatment of securities held by a bank.)
- **Disposition of market discount bonds.**—See section 1276 for rules on the disposition of any market discount bonds issued after July 18, 1984.
- **Capital gain distributions.**—Report capital gain distributions paid by mutual funds as long-term capital gains on line 5 regardless of how long the corporation owned stock in the fund.

Determining the Cost or Other Basis of Property

In determining gain or loss, the basis of property will generally be its cost. See section 1012 and the related regulations. Exceptions to the general rule are provided in sections in subchapters C, K, O, and P of the Code. For example, if the corporation acquired the property by dividend, liquidation of a corporation, transfer from a shareholder, reorganization, bequest, contribution or gift, tax-free exchange, involuntary conversion, certain asset acquisitions, or wash sale of stock, see sections 301 (or 1059), 334, 362 (or 358), 1014, 1015, 1031, 1033, 1060, and 1091, respectively. Attach an explanation if the corporation uses a basis other than actual cash cost of the property.

If the corporation is allowed a charitable contribution deduction because it sold property to a charitable organization, figure the adjusted basis for determining gain from the sale by dividing the amount realized by the fair market value and multiplying that result by the adjusted basis.

★U.S.GPO:1991-0-285-249

APPENDIXES

APPENDIX I

IRS FORMS AND INSTRUCTIONS

OTHER MATERIALS OF INTEREST AVAILABLE FROM THE IRS

Instructions for Form W-2
Instructions for Form 940
Instructions for Form 940-EZ
Instructions for Forms 1099, 1098, 5498, W-2G

Instructions for Form 1120S

Instructions for Form 2553

Instructions for Form 4562

Form 1099-A:	Acquisition or Abandonment of Secured Property
Form 1099-INT:	Interest Income
Form 1099-R:	Distributions from Pensions, Annuities, Retirement or Profit-Sharing Plans, IRAs, Insurance Contracts
Form 1099-S:	Proceeds from Real Estate Transactions
Form 1128:	Application to Adopt, Change, or Retain a Tax Year
Form 4136:	Credit for Federal Tax on Fuels
Form 4562:	Depreciation and Amortization
Form 4626:	Alternative Minimum Tax—Corporations
Form 4797:	Sales of Business Property
Form 5500-C/R:	Return/Report on Employee Benefit Plan
Form 7004:	Application for Automatic Extension of Time to File Corporate Income Tax Return
Form 8716:	Election to Have a Tax Year Other Than a Required Tax Year
Form 8810:	Corporate Passive Activity Loss and Credit Limitations

Form **SS-4**
(Rev. April 1991)
Department of the Treasury
Internal Revenue Service

Application for Employer Identification Number

(For use by employers and others. Please read the attached instructions before completing this form.)

EIN

OMB No. 1545-0003
Expires 4-30-94

Please type or print clearly.

1 Name of applicant (True legal name) (See instructions.)

2 Trade name of business, if different from name in line 1 | 3 Executor, trustee, "care of" name

4a Mailing address (street address) (room, apt., or suite no.) | 5a Address of business (See instructions.)

4b City, state, and ZIP code | 5b City, state, and ZIP code

6 County and state where principal business is located

7 Name of principal officer, grantor, or general partner (See instructions.) ▶

8a Type of entity (Check only one box.) (See instructions.)
- ☐ Individual SSN
- ☐ REMIC
- ☐ Personal service corp.
- ☐ State/local government
- ☐ National guard
- ☐ Estate
- ☐ Plan administrator SSN
- ☐ Other corporation (specify)
- ☐ Federal government/military
- ☐ Church or church controlled organization
- ☐ Trust
- ☐ Partnership
- ☐ Farmers' cooperative
- ☐ Other nonprofit organization (specify) ______ If nonprofit organization enter GEN (if applicable) ______
- ☐ Other (specify) ▶

8b If a corporation, give name of foreign country (if applicable) or state in the U.S. where incorporated ▶ | Foreign country | State

9 Reason for applying (Check only one box.)
- ☐ Started new business
- ☐ Hired employees
- ☐ Created a pension plan (specify type) ▶
- ☐ Banking purpose (specify) ▶
- ☐ Changed type of organization (specify) ▶
- ☐ Purchased going business
- ☐ Created a trust (specify) ▶
- ☐ Other (specify) ▶

10 Date business started or acquired (Mo., day, year) (See instructions.) | 11 Enter closing month of accounting year. (See instructions.)

12 First date wages or annuities were paid or will be paid (Mo., day, year). **Note:** *If applicant is a withholding agent, enter date income will first be paid to nonresident alien. (Mo., day, year)* . . . . ▶

13 Enter highest number of employees expected in the next 12 months. **Note:** *If the applicant does not expect to have any employees during the period, enter "0."* . . . . ▶ | Nonagricultural | Agricultural | Household

14 Principal activity (See instructions.) ▶

15 Is the principal business activity manufacturing? . . . . ☐ **Yes** ☐ **No**
If "Yes," principal product and raw material used ▶

16 To whom are most of the products or services sold? Please check the appropriate box. ☐ Business (wholesale)
☐ Public (retail) ☐ Other (specify) ▶ ☐ N/A

17a Has the applicant ever applied for an identification number for this or any other business? . . . . ☐ **Yes** ☐ **No**
Note: *If "Yes," please complete lines 17b and 17c.*

17b If you checked the "Yes" box in line 17a, give applicant's true name and trade name, if different than name shown on prior application.

True name ▶ Trade name ▶

17c Enter approximate date, city, and state where the application was filed and the previous employer identification number if known.

Approximate date when filed (Mo., day, year)	City and state where filed	Previous EIN

Under penalties of perjury, I declare that I have examined this application, and to the best of my knowledge and belief, it is true, correct, and complete | Telephone number (include area code)

Name and title (Please type or print clearly.) ▶

Signature ▶ Date ▶

Note: *Do not write below this line. For official use only.*

Please leave blank ▶	Geo.	Ind.	Class	Size	Reason for applying

For Paperwork Reduction Act Notice, see attached instructions. Cat. No. 16055N Form **SS-4** (Rev. 4-91)

1 Control number		OMB No. 1545-0008	This information is being furnished to the Internal Revenue Service. If you are required to file a tax return, a negligence penalty or other sanction may be imposed on you if this income is taxable and you fail to report it.
2 Employer's name, address, and ZIP code		6 Statutory employee ☐ Deceased ☐ Pension plan ☐ Legal rep. ☐ 942 emp. ☐ Subtotal ☐ Deferred compensation ☐ Void ☐	
		7 Allocated tips	8 Advance EIC payment
		9 Federal income tax withheld	10 Wages, tips, other compensation
3 Employer's identification number	4 Employer's state I.D. number	11 Social security tax withheld	12 Social security wages
5 Employee's social security number		13 Social security tips	14 Medicare wages and tips
19 Employee's name, address, and ZIP code		15 Medicare tax withheld	16 Nonqualified plans
		17 See Instrs. for Box 17	18 Other
20	21	22 Dependent care benefits	23 Benefits included in Box 10

24 State income tax	25 State wages, tips, etc.	26 Name of state	27 Local income tax	28 Local wages, tips, etc.	29 Name of locality

Copy C For EMPLOYEE'S RECORDS (See Notice on back.)

Department of the Treasury—Internal Revenue Service

Form W-2 Wage and Tax Statement 1991

1 Control number		OMB No. 1545-0008	This information is being furnished to the Internal Revenue Service. If you are required to file a tax return, a negligence penalty or other sanction may be imposed on you if this income is taxable and you fail to report it.
2 Employer's name, address, and ZIP code		6 Statutory employee ☐ Deceased ☐ Pension plan ☐ Legal rep. ☐ 942 emp. ☐ Subtotal ☐ Deferred compensation ☐ Void ☐	
		7 Allocated tips	8 Advance EIC payment
		9 Federal income tax withheld	10 Wages, tips, other compensation
3 Employer's identification number	4 Employer's state I.D. number	11 Social security tax withheld	12 Social security wages
5 Employee's social security number		13 Social security tips	14 Medicare wages and tips
19 Employee's name, address, and ZIP code		15 Medicare tax withheld	16 Nonqualified plans
		17 See Instrs. for Box 17	18 Other
20	21	22 Dependent care benefits	23 Benefits included in Box 10

24 State income tax	25 State wages, tips, etc.	26 Name of state	27 Local income tax	28 Local wages, tips, etc.	29 Name of locality

Copy C For EMPLOYEE'S RECORDS (See Notice on back.)

Department of the Treasury—Internal Revenue Service

Form W-2 Wage and Tax Statement 1991

Form **940**

Department of the Treasury
Internal Revenue Service

Employer's Annual Federal Unemployment (FUTA) Tax Return

▶ For Paperwork Reduction Act Notice, see separate instructions.

OMB No. 1545-0028

1991

EMPLOYER'S COPY

Employer identification number

A Did you pay all required contributions to state unemployment funds by the due date of Form 940? (If a 0% experience rate is granted, check "Yes" and see instructions.) . . . ☐ Yes ☐ No
If you checked the "Yes" box, enter the amount of contributions paid to state unemployment funds . ▶ $ ....

B Are you required to pay contributions to only one state? . . . ☐ Yes ☐ No
If you checked the "Yes" box: (1) Enter the name of the state where you have to pay contributions ▶ ....
(2) Enter your state reporting number(s) as shown on state unemployment tax return. ▶ ....
If you checked the "No" box, be sure to complete Part III and see the instructions.

C If any part of wages taxable for FUTA tax is exempt from state unemployment tax, check the box. (See the instructions.). . . . ☐

If you will not have to file returns in the future, check here, complete, and sign the return . . . ▶ ☐
If this is an Amended Return, check here . . . ▶ ☐

Part I **Computation of Taxable Wages** *(to be completed by all taxpayers)*

		Amount paid		
1	Total payments (including exempt payments) during the calendar year for services of employees.		1	
2	Exempt payments. (Explain each exemption shown, attach additional sheets if necessary.) ▶	2		
3	Payments of more than $7,000 for services. Enter only the amounts over the first $7,000 paid to each employee. Do not include payments from line 2. Do not use the state wage limitation . . .	3		
4	Total exempt payments (add lines 2 and 3). . . .		4	
5	**Total taxable wages** (subtract line 4 from line 1). . . . ▶		5	
6	Additional tax resulting from credit reduction for unrepaid advances to the state of Michigan. Enter the wages included on line 5 above for that state and multiply by the rate shown. (See the instructions.) Enter the credit reduction amount here and in Part II, line 2, or Part III, line 5: Michigan wages × .008 = . . . ▶		6	

Form **940** (1991)

Form 940 (1991) Page 4

Part II **Tax Due or Refund** *(Complete if you checked the "Yes" boxes in both questions A and B and did not check the box in C.)*

1	**FUTA tax.** Multiply the wages in Part I, line 5, by .008 and enter here	1	
2	Enter amount from Part I, line 6	2	
3	**Total FUTA tax** (add lines 1 and 2) ▶	3	
4	Total FUTA tax deposited for the year, including any overpayment applied from a prior year	4	
5	**Balance due** (subtract line 4 from line 3). This should be $100 or less. Pay to the Internal Revenue Service ▶	5	
6	**Overpayment** (subtract line 3 from line 4). Check if it is to be: ☐ **Applied to next return,** or ☐ **Refunded** ▶	6	

Part III **Tax Due or Refund** *(Complete if you checked the "No" box in either question A or B or you checked the box in C.)*

1	Gross FUTA tax. Multiply the wages in Part I, line 5, by .062	1	
2	Maximum credit. Multiply the wages in Part I, line 5, by .054 — 2		
3	Computation of tentative credit		

(a) Name of state	(b) State reporting number(s) as shown on employer's state contribution returns	(c) Taxable payroll (as defined in state act)	(d) State experience rate From	To	(e) State experience rate	(f) Contributions if rate had been 5.4% (col. (c) x .054)	(g) Contributions payable at experience rate (col. (c) x col. (e))	(h) Additional credit (col. (f) minus col.(g)). If 0 or less, enter 0.	(i) Contributions actually paid to the state
3a Totals ▶									

3b	**Total tentative credit** (add line 3a, columns (h) and (i) only—see instructions for limitations on late payments) ▶		
4	**Credit:** Enter the smaller of the amount in Part III, line 2, or line 3b — 4		
5	Enter the amount from Part I, line 6	5	
6	**Credit allowable** (subtract line 5 from line 4). (If zero or less, enter 0.)	6	
7	**Total FUTA tax** (subtract line 6 from line 1)	7	
8	Total FUTA tax deposited for the year, including any overpayment applied from a prior year	8	
9	**Balance due** (subtract line 8 from line 7). This should be $100 or less. Pay to the Internal Revenue Service ▶	9	
10	**Overpayment** (subtract line 7 from line 8). Check if it is to be: ☐ **Applied to next return,** or ☐ **Refunded** ▶	10	

Part IV **Record of Quarterly Federal Tax Liability for Unemployment Tax** *(Do not include state liability)*

Quarter	First	Second	Third	Fourth	Total for year
Liability for quarter					

Under penalties of perjury, I declare that I have examined this return, including accompanying schedules and statements, and to the best of my knowledge and belief, it is true, correct, and complete, and that no part of any payment made to a state unemployment fund claimed as a credit was or is to be deducted from the payments to employees.

Signature ▶ **Title (Owner, etc.) ▶** **Date ▶**

Note: *You must keep this copy and a copy of each related schedule or statement for 4 years after the date the tax is due or paid, whichever is later. These copies must be available for inspection by the IRS. See* **Circular E,** *Employer's Tax Guide, and* **Pub. 937,** *Business Reporting, for more information. Household employers should see* **Pub. 926,** *Employment Taxes for Household Employers.*

★U.S.GPO:1991-0-285-098

Form **940-EZ**

Department of the Treasury
Internal Revenue Service

Employer's Annual Federal Unemployment (FUTA) Tax Return

OMB No. 1545-1110

1991

If incorrect, make any necessary changes.

DD 10-1234567 9112 S28 B
Peter Cone
362 Main Street
Anytown VA 23000

Calendar year

Employer identification number

T	
FF	
FD	
FP	
I	
T	

Follow the chart under "Who Can Use Form 940-EZ" on page 2. If you cannot use Form 940-EZ, you must use Form 940 instead.

A Enter the amount of contributions paid to your state unemployment fund. (See instructions for line A on page 4.) ▶ $ 630.00

B (1) Enter the name of the state where you have to pay contributions ▶ Virginia

(2) Enter your state reporting number(s) as shown on state unemployment tax return. ▶ 98765432

If you will not have to file returns in the future, check here (see *Who Must File a Return* on page 2) **complete, and sign the return** ▶ ☐

If this is an Amended Return check here ▶ ☐

Part I Taxable Wages and FUTA Tax

		Amount paid	Line	
1	Total payments (including payments shown on lines 2 and 3) during the calendar year for services of employees		1	78,000.00
2	Exempt payments. (Explain all exempt payments, attaching additional sheets if necessary.) ▶	2		
3	Payments for services of more than $7,000. Enter only amounts over the first $7,000 paid to each employee. Do not include any exempt payments from line 2	3 57,000.00		
4	Total exempt payments (add lines 2 and 3)		4	57,000.00
5	**Total taxable wages** (subtract line 4 from line 1) ▶		5	21,000.00
6	**FUTA tax.** Multiply the wages on line 5 by .008 and enter here. (If the result is over $100, also complete Part II.)		6	168.00
7	Total FUTA tax deposited for the year, including any overpayment applied from a prior year (from your records)		7	142.40
8	**Amount you owe** (subtract line 7 from line 6). This should be $100 or less. Pay to "Internal Revenue Service". ▶		8	25.60
9	**Overpayment** (subtract line 6 from line 7). Check if it is to be: ☐ **Applied to next return, or** ☐ **Refunded** ▶		9	

Part II Record of Quarterly Federal Unemployment Tax Liability (Do not include state liability.) Complete only if line 6 is over $100.

Quarter	First (Jan. 1 - Mar. 31)	Second (Apr. 1 - June 30)	Third (July 1 - Sept. 30)	Fourth (Oct. 1 - Dec. 31)	Total for Year
Liability for quarter	142.40	25.60			168.00

Under penalties of perjury, I declare that I have examined this return, including accompanying schedules and statements, and, to the best of my knowledge and belief, it is true, correct, and complete, and that no part of any payment made to a state unemployment fund claimed as a credit was, or is to be, deducted from the payments to employees.

Signature ▶ Peter Cone   Title (Owner, etc.) ▶ Owner   Date ▶ 1-24-92

Form **941** (Rev. January 1991) Department of the Treasury Internal Revenue Service

4141

Employer's Quarterly Federal Tax Return

▶ See Circular E for more information concerning employment tax returns.

Please type or print.

Your name, address, employer identification number, and calendar quarter of return. (If not correct, please change.) ▶

DD 10-1234567 9112 S28 B
Peter Cone
362 Main Street
Anytown VA 23000

OMB No. 1545-0029
Expires: 5-31-93

T
FF
FD
FP
I
T

If address is different from prior return, check here ▶ ☐

IRS Use

If you do not have to file returns in the future, check here . . . ▶ ☐ Date final wages paid . . . ▶

If you are a seasonal employer, see **Seasonal employers** on page 2 and check here . ▶ ☐

Line	Description		Box	Amount
1a	Number of employees (except household) employed in the pay period that includes March 12th . ▶		1a	
b	If you are a subsidiary corporation AND your parent corporation files a consolidated Form 1120, enter parent corporation employer identification number (EIN) . . ▶ 1b –			
2	Total wages and tips subject to withholding, plus other compensation . . . . ▶		2	19,500 00
3	Total income tax withheld from wages, tips, pensions, annuities, sick pay, gambling, etc. . . ▶		3	2,158 00
4	Adjustment of withheld income tax for preceding quarters of calendar year (see instructions) . . ▶		4	
5	Adjusted total of income tax withheld (line 3 as adjusted by line 4—see instructions)		5	2,158 00
6a	Taxable social security wages (Complete line 7)	$ 19,500 00 × 12.4% (.124) =	6a	2,418 00
b	Taxable social security tips	$ × 12.4% (.124) =	6b	
7	Taxable Medicare wages and tips	$ 19,500 00 × 2.9% (.029) =	7	565 50
8	Total social security and Medicare taxes (add lines 6a, 6b, and 7)		8	2,983 50
9	Adjustment of social security and Medicare taxes (see instructions for required explanation) . . .		9	
10	Adjusted total of social security and Medicare taxes (line 8 as adjusted by line 9—see instructions) ▶		10	2,983 50
11	Backup withholding (see instructions)		11	
12	Adjustment of backup withholding tax for preceding quarters of calendar year. . . . . . . ▶		12	
13	Adjusted total of backup withholding (line 11 as adjusted by line 12)		13	
14	**Total taxes** (add lines 5, 10, and 13)		14	5,141 50
15	Advance earned income credit (EIC) payments made to employees, if any . . . . ▶		15	
16	Net taxes (subtract line 15 from line 14). **This should equal line IV below** (plus line IV of Schedule A (Form 941) if you have treated backup withholding as a separate liability)		16	5,141 50
17	**Total deposits for quarter,** including overpayment applied from a prior quarter, from your records. ▶		17	5,141 50
18	**Balance due** (subtract line 17 from line 16). This should be less than $500. Pay to IRS . . . . ▶		18	
19	**Overpayment,** if line 17 is more than line 16, enter here ▶ $ ________ and check if to be: ☐ Applied to next return **OR** ☐ Refunded.			

Record of Federal Tax Liability (You must complete if line 16 is $500 or more and Schedule B is not attached.) See instructions before checking these boxes.

Check only if you made deposits using the 95% rule ▶ ☐ Check only if you are a first time 3-banking-day depositor. . . ▶ ☐

Show tax liability here, **not deposits.** IRS gets deposit data from FTD coupons.

Date wages paid		First month of quarter		Second month of quarter		Third month of quarter
1st through 3rd	A		I		Q	
4th through 7th	B		J		R	
8th through 11th	C		K		S	
12th through 15th	D		L		T	
16th through 19th	E		M		U	
20th through 22nd	F		N		V	
23rd through 25th	G		O		W	
26th through the last	H		P		X	
Total liability for month	I	1,582.00	II	1,582.00	III	1,977.50

Do NOT Show Federal Tax Deposits Here

▶ *IV* Total for quarter (add lines *I*, *II*, and *III*). **This should equal line 16 above** . . . . ▶ 5,141.50

Sign Here

Under penalties of perjury, I declare that I have examined this return, including accompanying schedules and statements, and to the best of my knowledge and belief, it is true, correct, and complete.

Signature ▶ Peter Cone Print Your Name and Title ▶ Peter Cone Owner Date ▶ 2-6-92

For Paperwork Reduction Act Notice, see page 2.

DO NOT STAPLE 6969 ☐ CORRECTED

Form **1096** Department of the Treasury Internal Revenue Service

Annual Summary and Transmittal of U.S. Information Returns

OMB No. 1545-0108 **1991**

ATTACH IRS LABEL HERE

Type or machine print FILER'S name (or attach label)

Street address (room or suite number)

City, state, and ZIP code

If you are not using a preprinted label, enter in Box 1 or 2 below the identification number you used as the filer on the information returns being transmitted. Do not fill in both Boxes 1 and 2.

Name of person to contact if IRS needs more information

Telephone number ( )

For Official Use Only

1 Employer identification number	2 Social security number	3 Total number of documents	4 Federal income tax withheld	5 Total amount reported with this Form 1096
			$	$

Check only one box below to indicate the type of form being transmitted. If this is your FINAL return, check here . . . . ▶ ☐

☐	☐	☐	☐	☐	☐	☐	☐	☐	☐	☐	☐	☐
W-2G 32	1098 81	1099-A 80	1099-B 79	1099-DIV 91	1099-G 86	1099-INT 92	1099-MISC 95	1099-OID 96	1099-PATR 97	1099-R 98	1099-S 75	5498 28

Under penalties of perjury, I declare that I have examined this return and accompanying documents, and, to the best of my knowledge and belief, they are true, correct, and complete.

Signature ▶ .... Title ▶ .... Date ▶ ....

Please return this entire page to the Internal Revenue Service. Photocopies are NOT acceptable.

Instructions

Purpose of Form.—Use this form to transmit paper Forms 1099, 1098, 5498, and W-2G to the Internal Revenue Service. DO NOT USE FORM 1096 TO TRANSMIT MAGNETIC MEDIA. See **Form 4804,** Transmittal of Information Returns Reported on Magnetic Media.

Use of Preprinted Label.—If you received a preprinted label from IRS with Package 1099, place the label in the name and address area of this form inside the brackets. Make any necessary changes to your name and address on the label. However, do not use the label if the taxpayer identification number (TIN) shown is incorrect. **Do not prepare your own label. Use only the IRS-prepared label that came with your Package 1099.**

If you are not using a preprinted label, enter the filer's name, address (including room, suite, or other unit number), and TIN in the spaces provided on the form.

Filer.—The name, address, and TIN of the filer on this form must be the same as those you enter in the upper left area of Form 1099, 1098, 5498, or W-2G. A filer includes a payer, a recipient of mortgage interest payments, a broker, a barter exchange, a person reporting real estate transactions, a trustee or issuer of an individual retirement arrangement (including an IRA or SEP), and a lender who acquires an interest in secured property or who has reason to know that the property has been abandoned.

Transmitting to IRS.—Group the forms by form number and transmit each group with a **separate** Form 1096. For example, if you must file both Forms 1098 and Forms 1099-A, complete one Form 1096 to transmit your Forms 1098 and another Form 1096 to transmit your Forms 1099-A. Also submit a separate Form 1096 for each type of corrected form.

Box 1 or 2.—Complete only if you are not using a preprinted IRS label. Individuals not in a trade or business must enter their social security number in Box 2; sole proprietors and all others must enter their employer identification number in Box 1. However, sole proprietors who are not required to have an employer identification number must enter their social security number in Box 2.

Box 3.—Enter the number of forms you are transmitting with this Form 1096. Do not include blank or voided forms or the Form 1096 in your total. Enter the number of correctly completed forms, not the number of pages, being transmitted. For example, if you send one page of three-to-a-page Forms 5498 with a Form 1096 and you have correctly completed two Forms 5498 on that page, enter 2 in Box 3 of Form 1096.

Box 4.—Enter the total Federal income tax withheld shown on the forms being transmitted with this Form 1096.

Box 5.—No entry is required if you are filing Form 1099-A or 1099-G. For all other forms, enter the total of the amounts from the specific boxes of the forms listed below:

Form	Boxes
Form W-2G	Box 1
Form 1098	Boxes 1 and 2
Form 1099-B	Boxes 2 and 3
Form 1099-DIV	Boxes 1a, 5, and 6
Form 1099-INT	Boxes 1 and 3
Form 1099-MISC	Boxes 1, 2, 3, 5, 6, 7, 8, and 10
Form 1099-OID	Boxes 1 and 2
Form 1099-PATR	Boxes 1, 2, 3, and 5
Form 1099-R	Box 1
Form 1099-S	Box 2
Form 5498	Boxes 1 and 2

For Paperwork Reduction Act Notice, see the separate Instructions for Forms 1099, 1098, 5498, and W-2G. Form **1096** (1991)

FORM 1099-DIV

☐ VOID ☐ CORRECTED

PAYER'S name, street address, city, state, and ZIP code			1a Gross dividends and other distributions on stock (Total of 1b, 1c, 1d, and 1e) $ 1b Ordinary dividends $	OMB No. 1545-0110 1991	Dividends and Distributions
PAYER'S Federal identification number	RECIPIENT'S identification number		1c Capital gain distributions $	2 Federal income tax withheld $	Copy C For Payer For Paperwork Reduction Act Notice and instructions for completing this form, see Instructions for Forms 1099, 1098, 5498, and W-2G.
RECIPIENT'S name			1d Nontaxable distributions $	3 Foreign tax paid $	
Street address (including apt. no.)			1e Investment expenses $	4 Foreign country or U.S. possession	
City, state, and ZIP code			Liquidation Distributions		
Account number (optional)		2nd TIN Not. ☐	5 Cash $	6 Noncash (Fair market value) $	

Form 1099-DIV Department of the Treasury - Internal Revenue Service

☐ VOID ☐ CORRECTED

PAYER'S name, street address, city, state, and ZIP code			1a Gross dividends and other distributions on stock (Total of 1b, 1c, 1d, and 1e) $ 1b Ordinary dividends $	OMB No. 1545-0110 1991	Dividends and Distributions
PAYER'S Federal identification number	RECIPIENT'S identification number		1c Capital gain distributions $	2 Federal income tax withheld $	Copy C For Payer For Paperwork Reduction Act Notice and instructions for completing this form, see Instructions for Forms 1099, 1098, 5498, and W-2G.
RECIPIENT'S name			1d Nontaxable distributions $	3 Foreign tax paid $	
Street address (including apt. no.)			1e Investment expenses $	4 Foreign country or U.S. possession	
City, state, and ZIP code			Liquidation Distributions		
Account number (optional)		2nd TIN Not. ☐	5 Cash $	6 Noncash (Fair market value) $	

Form 1099-DIV Department of the Treasury - Internal Revenue Service

☐ VOID ☐ CORRECTED

PAYER'S name, street address, city, state, and ZIP code			1a Gross dividends and other distributions on stock (Total of 1b, 1c, 1d, and 1e) $ 1b Ordinary dividends $	OMB No. 1545-0110 1991	Dividends and Distributions
PAYER'S Federal identification number	RECIPIENT'S identification number		1c Capital gain distributions $	2 Federal income tax withheld $	Copy C For Payer For Paperwork Reduction Act Notice and instructions for completing this form, see Instructions for Forms 1099, 1098, 5498, and W-2G.
RECIPIENT'S name			1d Nontaxable distributions $	3 Foreign tax paid $	
Street address (including apt. no.)			1e Investment expenses $	4 Foreign country or U.S. possession	
City, state, and ZIP code			Liquidation Distributions		
Account number (optional)		2nd TIN Not. ☐	5 Cash $	6 Noncash (Fair market value) $	

Form 1099-DIV Department of the Treasury - Internal Revenue Service

FORM 1099-MISC

☐ CORRECTED (if checked)

PAYER'S name, street address, city, state, and ZIP code		1 Rents $	OMB No. 1545-0115	Miscellaneous Income
		2 Royalties $	1991	
		3 Prizes, awards, etc. $		
PAYER'S Federal identification number	RECIPIENT'S identification number	4 Federal income tax withheld $	5 Fishing boat proceeds $	Copy 2 To be filed with recipient's state income tax return, when required.
RECIPIENT'S name		6 Medical and health care payments $	7 Nonemployee compensation $	
Street address (including apt. no.)		8 Substitute payments in lieu of dividends or interest $	9 Payer made direct sales of $5,000 or more of consumer products to a buyer (recipient) for resale ▶ ☐	
City, state, and ZIP code		10 Crop insurance proceeds $	11 State income tax withheld $	
Account number (optional)		12 State/Payer's state number		

Form **1099-MISC** Department of the Treasury - Internal Revenue Service

☐ CORRECTED (if checked)

PAYER'S name, street address, city, state, and ZIP code		1 Rents $	OMB No. 1545-0115	Miscellaneous Income
		2 Royalties $	1991	
		3 Prizes, awards, etc. $		
PAYER'S Federal identification number	RECIPIENT'S identification number	4 Federal income tax withheld $	5 Fishing boat proceeds $	Copy 2 To be filed with recipient's state income tax return, when required.
RECIPIENT'S name		6 Medical and health care payments $	7 Nonemployee compensation $	
Street address (including apt. no.)		8 Substitute payments in lieu of dividends or interest $	9 Payer made direct sales of $5,000 or more of consumer products to a buyer (recipient) for resale ▶ ☐	
City, state, and ZIP code		10 Crop insurance proceeds $	11 State income tax withheld $	
Account number (optional)		12 State/Payer's state number		

Form **1099-MISC** Department of the Treasury - Internal Revenue Service

☐ CORRECTED (if checked)

PAYER'S name, street address, city, state, and ZIP code		1 Rents $	OMB No. 1545-0115	Miscellaneous Income
		2 Royalties $	1991	
		3 Prizes, awards, etc. $		
PAYER'S Federal identification number	RECIPIENT'S identification number	4 Federal income tax withheld $	5 Fishing boat proceeds $	Copy 2 To be filed with recipient's state income tax return, when required.
RECIPIENT'S name		6 Medical and health care payments $	7 Nonemployee compensation $	
Street address (including apt. no.)		8 Substitute payments in lieu of dividends or interest $	9 Payer made direct sales of $5,000 or more of consumer products to a buyer (recipient) for resale ▶ ☐	
City, state, and ZIP code		10 Crop insurance proceeds $	11 State income tax withheld $	
Account number (optional)		12 State/Payer's state number		

Form **1099-MISC** Department of the Treasury - Internal Revenue Service

Form **1120S**
Department of the Treasury
Internal Revenue Service

U.S. Income Tax Return for an S Corporation

For calendar year 1991, or tax year beginning ...., 1991, and ending ...., 19 .....
▶ See separate instructions.

OMB No. 1545-0130

1991

A Date of election as an S corporation	**Use IRS label. Otherwise, please print or type.**	Name	**C Employer identification number**
		Number, street, and room or suite no. (If a P.O. box, see page 8 of the instructions.)	D Date incorporated
B Business code no. (see Specific Instructions)		City or town, state, and ZIP code	E Total assets (see Specific Instructions) $

F Check applicable boxes: (1) ☐ Initial return (2) ☐ Final return (3) ☐ Change in address (4) ☐ Amended return

G Check this box if this S corporation is subject to the consolidated audit procedures of sections 6241 through 6245 (see instructions before checking this box) . ▶ ☐

H Enter number of shareholders in the corporation at end of the tax year . . . . . ▶

Caution: *Include **only** trade or business income and expenses on lines 1a through 21. See the instructions for more information.*

Income	1a	Gross receipts or sales		**b** Less returns and allowances ___ **c** Bal ▶	1c	
	2	Cost of goods sold (Schedule A, line 8)			2	
	3	Gross profit. Subtract line 2 from line 1c			3	
	4	Net gain (loss) from Form 4797, Part II, line 18 *(attach Form 4797)*			4	
	5	Other income (see instructions) *(attach schedule)*			5	
	6	**Total income (loss).** Combine lines 3 through 5 ▶			6	
Deductions (See instructions for limitations.)	7	Compensation of officers			7	
	8a	Salaries and wages		**b** Less jobs credit ___ **c** Bal ▶	8c	
	9	Repairs			9	
	10	Bad debts			10	
	11	Rents			11	
	12	Taxes			12	
	13	Interest			13	
	14a	Depreciation (see instructions)	14a			
	b	Depreciation claimed on Schedule A and elsewhere on return	14b			
	c	Subtract line 14b from line 14a			14c	
	15	Depletion **(Do not deduct oil and gas depletion.)**			15	
	16	Advertising			16	
	17	Pension, profit-sharing, etc., plans			17	
	18	Employee benefit programs			18	
	19	Other deductions *(attach schedule)*			19	
	20	**Total deductions.** Add lines 7 through 19 ▶			20	
	21	Ordinary income (loss) from trade or business activities. Subtract line 20 from line 6			21	
Tax and Payments	22	**Tax:**				
	a	Excess net passive income tax *(attach schedule)*	22a			
	b	Tax from Schedule D (Form 1120S)	22b			
	c	Add lines 22a and 22b (see instructions for additional taxes)			22c	
	23	**Payments:**				
	a	1991 estimated tax payments	23a			
	b	Tax deposited with Form 7004	23b			
	c	Credit for Federal tax on fuels *(attach Form 4136)*	23c			
	d	Add lines 23a through 23c			23d	
	24	Estimated tax penalty (see page 3 of instructions). Check if Form 2220 is attached ▶ ☐			24	
	25	**Tax due.** If the total of lines 22c and 24 is larger than line 23d, enter amount owed. See instructions for depositary method of payment ▶			25	
	26	**Overpayment.** If line 23d is larger than the total of lines 22c and 24, enter amount overpaid ▶			26	
	27	Enter amount of line 26 you want: **Credited to 1992 estimated tax ▶**		**Refunded ▶**	27	

Please Sign Here

Under penalties of perjury, I declare that I have examined this return, including accompanying schedules and statements, and to the best of my knowledge and belief, it is true, correct, and complete. Declaration of preparer (other than taxpayer) is based on all information of which preparer has any knowledge.

▶ Signature of officer | Date | ▶ Title

Paid Preparer's Use Only

Preparer's signature ▶		Date	Check if self-employed ▶ ☐	Preparer's social security number
Firm's name (or yours if self-employed) and address ▶			E.I. No. ▶	
			ZIP code ▶	

For Paperwork Reduction Act Notice, see page 1 of separate instructions. Cat. No. 11510H Form **1120S** (1991)

Form 1120S (1991) Page 2

Schedule A **Cost of Goods Sold** (See instructions.)

1	Inventory at beginning of year	1	
2	Purchases	2	
3	Cost of labor	3	
4	Additional section 263A costs (see instructions) *(attach schedule)*	4	
5	Other costs *(attach schedule)*.	5	
6	**Total.** Add lines 1 through 5	6	
7	Inventory at end of year	7	
8	**Cost of goods sold.** Subtract line 7 from line 6. Enter here and on line 2, page 1	8	

9a Check all methods used for valuing closing inventory:

(i) ☐ Cost

(ii) ☐ Lower of cost or market as described in Regulations section 1.471-4

(iii) ☐ Writedown of "subnormal" goods as described in Regulations section 1.471-2(c)

(iv) ☐ Other (specify method used and attach explanation) ▶ ....

b Check if the LIFO inventory method was adopted this tax year for any goods *(if checked, attach Form 970)*. ▶ ☐

c If the LIFO inventory method was used for this tax year, enter percentage (or amounts) of closing inventory computed under LIFO . . . **9c** ______

d Do the rules of section 263A (for property produced or acquired for resale) apply to the corporation? ☐ Yes ☐ No

e Was there any change in determining quantities, cost, or valuations between opening and closing inventory? ☐ Yes ☐ No
If "Yes," attach explanation.

Schedule B **Other Information**

		Yes	No
1	Check method of accounting: **(a)** ☐ Cash **(b)** ☐ Accrual **(c)** ☐ Other (specify) ▶		
2	Refer to the list in the instructions and state your principal: **(a)** Business activity ▶ .... **(b)** Product or service ▶		
3	Did you at the end of the tax year own, directly or indirectly, 50% or more of the voting stock of a domestic corporation? (For rules of attribution, see section 267(c).) If "Yes," attach a schedule showing: **(a)** name, address, and employer identification number and **(b)** percentage owned.		
4	Were you a member of a controlled group subject to the provisions of section 1561?		
5	At any time during the tax year, did you have an interest in or a signature or other authority over a financial account in a foreign country (such as a bank account, securities account, or other financial account)? (See instructions for exceptions and filing requirements for form TD F 90-22.1.) If "Yes," enter the name of the foreign country ▶		
6	Were you the grantor of, or transferor to, a foreign trust that existed during the current tax year, whether or not you have any beneficial interest in it? If "Yes," you may have to file Forms 3520, 3520-A, or 926		
7	Check this box if the corporation has filed or is required to file **Form 8264,** Application for Registration of a Tax Shelter ▶ ☐		
8	Check this box if the corporation issued publicly offered debt instruments with original issue discount ▶ ☐ If so, the corporation may have to file **Form 8281,** Information Return for Publicly Offered Original Issue Discount Instruments.		
9	If the corporation: **(a)** filed its election to be an S corporation after 1986, **(b)** was a C corporation before it elected to be an S corporation **or** the corporation acquired an asset with a basis determined by reference to its basis (or the basis of any other property) in the hands of a C corporation, and **(c)** has net unrealized built-in gain (defined in section 1374(d)(1)) in excess of the net recognized built-in gain from prior years, enter the net unrealized built-in gain reduced by net recognized built-in gain from prior years (see instructions) ▶ $..........		
10	Check this box if the corporation had subchapter C earnings and profits at the close of the tax year (see instructions) ▶ ☐		

Designation of Tax Matters Person (See instructions.)

Enter below the shareholder designated as the tax matters person (TMP) for the tax year of this return:

Name of designated TMP ▶ __________ Identifying number of TMP ▶ __________

Address of designated TMP ▶ __________

Form 1120S (1991) Page 3

Schedule K Shareholders' Shares of Income, Credits, Deductions, etc.

	(a) Pro rata share items		(b) Total amount
Income (Loss)	1 Ordinary income (loss) from trade or business activities (page 1, line 21)	1	
	2 Net income (loss) from rental real estate activities *(attach Form 8825)*	2	
	3a Gross income from other rental activities . . . 3a		
	b Less expenses *(attach schedule)*. . . 3b		
	c Net income (loss) from other rental activities	3c	
	4 Portfolio income (loss):		
	a Interest income	4a	
	b Dividend income	4b	
	c Royalty income	4c	
	d Net short-term capital gain (loss) *(attach Schedule D (Form 1120S))*	4d	
	e Net long-term capital gain (loss) *(attach Schedule D (Form 1120S))*	4e	
	f Other portfolio income (loss) *(attach schedule)*	4f	
	5 Net gain (loss) under section 1231 (other than due to casualty or theft) *(attach Form 4797)*	5	
	6 Other income (loss) *(attach schedule)*	6	
Deductions	7 Charitable contributions (see instructions) *(attach list)*	7	
	8 Section 179 expense deduction *(attach Form 4562)*	8	
	9 Deductions related to portfolio income (loss) (see instructions) (itemize)	9	
	10 Other deductions *(attach schedule)*	10	
Investment Interest	11a Interest expense on investment debts	11a	
	b (1) Investment income included on lines 4a through 4f above	11b(1)	
	(2) Investment expenses included on line 9 above	11b(2)	
Credits	12a Credit for alcohol used as a fuel *(attach Form 6478)*	12a	
	b Low-income housing credit (see instructions):		
	(1) From partnerships to which section 42(j)(5) applies for property placed in service before 1990	12b(1)	
	(2) Other than on line 12b(1) for property placed in service before 1990	12b(2)	
	(3) From partnerships to which section 42(j)(5) applies for property placed in service after 1989	12b(3)	
	(4) Other than on line 12b(3) for property placed in service after 1989	12b(4)	
	c Qualified rehabilitation expenditures related to rental real estate activities *(attach Form 3468)*	12c	
	d Credits (other than credits shown on lines 12b and 12c) related to rental real estate activities (see instructions)	12d	
	e Credits related to other rental activities (see instructions)	12e	
	13 Other credits (see instructions)	13	
Adjustments and Tax Preference Items	14a Accelerated depreciation of real property placed in service before 1987	14a	
	b Accelerated depreciation of leased personal property placed in service before 1987	14b	
	c Depreciation adjustment on property placed in service after 1986	14c	
	d Depletion (other than oil and gas)	14d	
	e (1) Gross income from oil, gas, or geothermal properties	14e(1)	
	(2) Deductions allocable to oil, gas, or geothermal properties	14e(2)	
	f Other adjustments and tax preference items *(attach schedule)*	14f	
Foreign Taxes	15a Type of income ▶		
	b Name of foreign country or U.S. possession ▶		
	c Total gross income from sources outside the United States *(attach schedule)*	15c	
	d Total applicable deductions and losses *(attach schedule)*	15d	
	e Total foreign taxes (check one): ▶ ☐ Paid ☐ Accrued	15e	
	f Reduction in taxes available for credit *(attach schedule)*	15f	
	g Other foreign tax information *(attach schedule)*	15g	
Other	16a Total expenditures to which a section 59(e) election may apply	16a	
	b Type of expenditures ▶		
	17 Total property distributions (including cash) other than dividends reported on line 19 below	17	
	18 Other items and amounts required to be reported separately to shareholders (see instructions) *(attach schedule)*		
	19 Total dividend distributions paid from accumulated earnings and profits	19	
	20 **Income (loss)** (Required only if Schedule M-1 must be completed.). Combine lines 1 through 6 in column (b). From the result, subtract the sum of lines 7 through 11a, 15e, and 16a	20	

Form 1120S (1991) Page 4

Schedule L Balance Sheets

Assets	Beginning of tax year (a)	(b)	End of tax year (c)	(d)
1 Cash				
2a Trade notes and accounts receivable				
b Less allowance for bad debts				
3 Inventories				
4 U.S. Government obligations				
5 Tax-exempt securities				
6 Other current assets *(attach schedule)*				
7 Loans to shareholders				
8 Mortgage and real estate loans				
9 Other investments *(attach schedule)*				
10a Buildings and other depreciable assets				
b Less accumulated depreciation				
11a Depletable assets				
b Less accumulated depletion				
12 Land (net of any amortization)				
13a Intangible assets (amortizable only)				
b Less accumulated amortization				
14 Other assets *(attach schedule)*				
15 Total assets				
Liabilities and Shareholders' Equity				
16 Accounts payable				
17 Mortgages, notes, bonds payable in less than 1 year				
18 Other current liabilities *(attach schedule)*				
19 Loans from shareholders				
20 Mortgages, notes, bonds payable in 1 year or more				
21 Other liabilities *(attach schedule)*				
22 Capital stock				
23 Paid-in or capital surplus				
24 Retained earnings				
25 Less cost of treasury stock		( )		( )
26 Total liabilities and shareholders' equity				

Schedule M-1 Reconciliation of Income per Books With Income per Return (You are not required to complete this schedule if the total assets on line 15, column (d), of Schedule L are less than $25,000.)

1 Net income per books		5 Income recorded on books this year not included on Schedule K, lines 1 through 6 (itemize): a Tax-exempt interest $	
2 Income included on Schedule K, lines 1 through 6, not recorded on books this year (itemize):			
3 Expenses recorded on books this year not included on Schedule K, lines 1 through 11a, 15e, and 16a (itemize): a Depreciation $ b Travel and entertainment $		6 Deductions included on Schedule K, lines 1 through 11a, 15e, and 16a, not charged against book income this year (itemize): a Depreciation $	
		7 Add lines 5 and 6	
4 Add lines 1 through 3		8 Income (loss) (Schedule K, line 20). Line 4 less line 7	

Schedule M-2 Analysis of Accumulated Adjustments Account, Other Adjustments Account, and Shareholders' Undistributed Taxable Income Previously Taxed (See instructions.)

	(a) Accumulated adjustments account	(b) Other adjustments account	(c) Shareholders' undistributed taxable income previously taxed
1 Balance at beginning of tax year			
2 Ordinary income from page 1, line 21			
3 Other additions			
4 Loss from page 1, line 21	( )		
5 Other reductions	( )	( )	
6 Combine lines 1 through 5			
7 Distributions other than dividend distributions			
8 Balance at end of tax year. Subtract line 7 from line 6			

*U.S. GPO:1991-285-273

SCHEDULE D (Form 1120S)

Department of the Treasury
Internal Revenue Service

Capital Gains and Losses and Built-In Gains

▶ Attach to Form 1120S.

▶ See separate instructions.

OMB No. 1545-0130

1991

Name	Employer identification number

Part I Short-Term Capital Gains and Losses—Assets Held One Year or Less

(a) Kind of property and description (Example, 100 shares of "Z" Co.)	(b) Date acquired (mo., day, yr.)	(c) Date sold (mo., day, yr.)	(d) Gross sales price	(e) Cost or other basis, plus expense of sale	(f) Gain or (loss) ((d) less (e))
1					

2	Short-term capital gain from installment sales from Form 6252, line 22 or 30	2	
3	**Net short-term capital gain or (loss).** Combine lines 1 and 2 and enter here. Also enter this amount on Form 1120S, Schedule K, line 4d or line 6 (but first reduce it by any tax on short-term gain included on line 23 below)	3	

Part II Long-Term Capital Gains and Losses—Assets Held More Than One Year

(a)	(b)	(c)	(d)	(e)	(f)
4					

5	Long-term capital gain from installment sales from Form 6252, line 22 or 30	5	
6	**Net long-term capital gain or (loss).** Combine lines 4 and 5 and enter here. Also enter this amount on Form 1120S, Schedule K, line 4e or line 6 (but first reduce it by any tax on long-term gain included on lines 15 and 23 below)	6	

Part III Capital Gains Tax (See instructions before completing this part.)

7	Enter section 1231 gain from Form 4797, line 9	7	
8	Net long-term capital gain or (loss)—Combine lines 6 and 7	8	
	Note: *If the corporation is liable for the excess net passive income tax (Form 1120S, page 1, line 22a) or the built-in gains tax (Part IV below), see the line 9 instructions before completing line 9.*		
9	Net capital gain—Enter excess of net long-term capital gain (line 8) over net short-term capital loss (line 3).	9	
10	Statutory minimum	10	$25,000
11	Subtract line 10 from line 9	11	
12	Enter 34% of line 11	12	
13	Taxable income (see instructions and attach computation schedule)	13	
14	Enter tax on line 13 amount (see instructions and attach computation schedule)	14	
15	**Tax.** Enter smaller of line 12 or line 14 here and on Form 1120S, page 1, line 22b	15	

Part IV Built-In Gains Tax (See instructions before completing this part.)

16	Excess of recognized built-in gains over recognized built-in losses (see instructions and attach computation schedule)	16	
17	Taxable income (see instructions and attach computation schedule)	17	
18	Net recognized built-in gain. Enter smaller of line 16 or line 17 (see instructions)	18	
19	Section 1374(b)(2) deduction	19	
20	Subtract line 19 from line 18. (If zero or less, enter zero here and on line 23.)	20	
21	Enter 34% of line 20	21	
22	Business credit and minimum tax credit carryforwards under section 1374(b)(3) from C corporation years	22	
23	**Tax.** Subtract line 22 from line 21 (if zero or less, enter -0-). Enter here and on Form 1120S, page 1, line 22b	23	

For Paperwork Reduction Act Notice, see page 1 of Instructions for Form 1120S. Cat. No. 11516V **Schedule D (Form 1120S) 1991**

★U.S.GPO:1991-0-285-275

SCHEDULE K-1 (Form 1120S)

Department of the Treasury
Internal Revenue Service

Shareholder's Share of Income, Credits, Deductions, etc.

▶ See separate instructions.

For calendar year 1991 or tax year beginning , 1991, and ending , 19

OMB No. 1545-0130

1991

Shareholder's identifying number ▶

Shareholder's name, address, and ZIP code

Corporation's identifying number ▶

Corporation's name, address, and ZIP code

A Shareholder's percentage of stock ownership for tax year (see Instructions for Schedule K-1) . . . . . . ▶ .... %

B Internal Revenue service center where corporation filed its return ▶ ....

C **(1)** Tax shelter registration number (see Instructions for Schedule K-1) . . . . ▶ ....

(2) Type of tax shelter ▶ ....

D Check applicable boxes: **(1)** ☐ Final K-1 **(2)** ☐ Amended K-1

		(a) Pro rata share items		**(b)** Amount	**(c)** Form 1040 filers enter the amount in column (b) on:
Income (Loss)	1	Ordinary income (loss) from trade or business activities	1		See Shareholder's Instructions for Schedule K-1 (Form 1120S).
	2	Net income (loss) from rental real estate activities	2		
	3	Net income (loss) from other rental activities	3		
	4	Portfolio income (loss):			
	a	Interest	4a		Sch. B, Part I, line 1
	b	Dividends	4b		Sch. B, Part II, line 5
	c	Royalties	4c		Sch. E, Part I, line 4
	d	Net short-term capital gain (loss)	4d		Sch. D, line 4, col. (f) or (g)
	e	Net long-term capital gain (loss)	4e		Sch. D, line 11, col. (f) or (g)
	f	Other portfolio income (loss) *(attach schedule)*	4f		(Enter on applicable line of your return.)
	5	Net gain (loss) under section 1231 (other than due to casualty or theft)	5		See Shareholder's Instructions for Schedule K-1 (Form 1120S).
	6	Other income (loss) *(attach schedule)*	6		(Enter on applicable line of your return.)
Deductions	7	Charitable contributions (see instructions) *(attach schedule)*	7		Sch. A, line 13 or 14
	8	Section 179 expense deduction	8		See Shareholder's Instructions for Schedule K-1 (Form 1120S).
	9	Deductions related to portfolio income (loss) *(attach schedule)*	9		
	10	Other deductions *(attach schedule)*	10		
Investment Interest	11a	Interest expense on investment debts	11a		Form 4952, line 1
	b	**(1)** Investment income included on lines 4a through 4f above	b(1)		See Shareholder's Instructions for Schedule K-1 (Form 1120S).
		(2) Investment expenses included on line 9 above	b(2)		
Credits	12a	Credit for alcohol used as fuel	12a		Form 6478, line 10
	b	Low-income housing credit:			
		(1) From section 42(j)(5) partnerships for property placed in service before 1990	b(1)		Form 8586, line 5
		(2) Other than on line 12b(1) for property placed in service before 1990	b(2)		
		(3) From section 42(j)(5) partnerships for property placed in service after 1989	b(3)		
		(4) Other than on line 12b(3) for property placed in service after 1989	b(4)		
	c	Qualified rehabilitation expenditures related to rental real estate activities (see instructions)	12c		See Shareholder's Instructions for Schedule K-1 (Form 1120S).
	d	Credits (other than credits shown on lines 12b and 12c) related to rental real estate activities (see instructions)	12d		
	e	Credits related to other rental activities (see instructions)	12e		
	13	Other credits (see instructions)	13		
Adjustments and Tax Preference Items	14a	Accelerated depreciation of real property placed in service before 1987	14a		See Shareholder's Instructions for Schedule K-1 (Form 1120S) and Instructions for Form 6251
	b	Accelerated depreciation of leased personal property placed in service before 1987	14b		
	c	Depreciation adjustment on property placed in service after 1986	14c		
	d	Depletion (other than oil and gas)	14d		
	e	**(1)** Gross income from oil, gas, or geothermal properties	e(1)		
		(2) Deductions allocable to oil, gas, or geothermal properties	e(2)		
	f	Other adjustments and tax preference items *(attach schedule)*	14f		

For Paperwork Reduction Act Notice, see page 1 of Instructions for Form 1120S. Cat. No. 11520D **Schedule K-1 (Form 1120S) 1991**

Schedule K-1 (Form 1120S) (1991) Page 2

	(a) Pro rata share items		(b) Amount	(c) Form 1040 filers enter the amount in column (b) on:
Foreign Taxes	15a Type of income ▶			Form 1116, Check boxes
	b Name of foreign country or U.S. possession ▶			Form 1116, Part I
	c Total gross income from sources outside the U.S. *(attach schedule)*	15c		
	d Total applicable deductions and losses *(attach schedule)*	15d		
	e Total foreign taxes (check one): ▶ ☐ Paid ☐ Accrued	15e		Form 1116, Part II
	f Reduction in taxes available for credit *(attach schedule)*	15f		Form 1116, Part III
	g Other foreign tax information *(attach schedule)*	15g		See Instructions for Form 1116
Other	16a Total expenditures to which a section 59(e) election may apply	16a		See Shareholder's Instructions for Schedule K-1 (Form 1120S).
	b Type of expenditures ▶			
	17 Property distributions (including cash) other than dividend distributions reported to you on Form 1099-DIV	17		
	18 Amount of loan repayments for "Loans From Shareholders"	18		
	19 Recapture of low-income housing credit:			
	a From section 42(j)(5) partnerships	19a		Form 8611, line 8
	b Other than on line 19a	19b		

Supplemental Information

20 Supplemental information required to be reported separately to each shareholder *(attach additional schedules if more space is needed)*:

*U.S. Government Printing Office: 1991 — 285-277

Form **2553**
(Rev. December 1990)
Department of the Treasury
Internal Revenue Service

Election by a Small Business Corporation

(Under section 1362 of the Internal Revenue Code)

▶ For Paperwork Reduction Act Notice, see page 1 of instructions.

▶ See separate instructions.

OMB No. 1545-0146
Expires 11-30-93

Notes: 1. *This election, to be treated as an "S corporation," can be accepted only if all the tests in General Instruction B are met; all signatures in Parts I and III are originals (no photocopies); and the exact name and address of the corporation and other required form information are provided.*

2. *Do not file Form 1120S until you are notified that your election is accepted. See General Instruction E.*

Part I Election Information

Please Type or Print

Name of corporation (see instructions)	**A Employer identification number** (see instructions)
Number, street, and room or suite no. (If a P.O. box, see instructions.)	**B** Name and telephone number (including area code) of corporate officer or legal representative who may be called for information
City or town, state, and ZIP code	**C** Election is to be effective for tax year beginning (month, day, year)

D Is the corporation the outgrowth or continuation of any form of predecessor? . . ☐ Yes ☐ No
If "Yes," state name of predecessor, type of organization, and period of its existence ▶

E Date of incorporation

F Check here ▶ ☐ if the corporation has changed its name or address since applying for the employer identification number shown in item A above.

G State of incorporation

H If this election takes effect for the first tax year the corporation exists, enter month, day, and year of the **earliest** of the following: (1) date the corporation first had shareholders, (2) date the corporation first had assets, or (3) date the corporation began doing business. ▶

I Selected tax year: Annual return will be filed for tax year ending (month and day) ▶
If the tax year ends on any date other than December 31, except for an automatic 52-53-week tax year ending with reference to the month of December, you **must** complete Part II on the back. If the date you enter is the ending date of an automatic 52-53-week tax year, write "52-53-week year" to the right of the date. See Temporary Regulations section 1.441-2T(e)(3).

J Name of each shareholder, person having a community property interest in the corporation's stock, and each tenant in common, joint tenant, and tenant by the entirety. (A husband and wife (and their estates) are counted as one shareholder in determining the number of shareholders without regard to the manner in which the stock is owned.)	**K** Shareholders' Consent Statement. We, the undersigned shareholders, consent to the corporation's election to be treated as an "S corporation" under section 1362(a). (Shareholders sign and date below.)*		**L** Stock owned		**M** Social security number or employer identification number (see instructions)	**N** Shareholder's tax year ends (month and day)
	Signature	Date	Number of shares	Dates acquired		

*For this election to be valid, the consent of each shareholder, person having a community property interest in the corporation's stock, and each tenant in common, joint tenant, and tenant by the entirety must either appear above or be attached to this form. (See instructions for Column K if continuation sheet or a separate consent statement is needed.)

Under penalties of perjury, I declare that I have examined this election, including accompanying schedules and statements, and to the best of my knowledge and belief, it is true, correct, and complete.

Signature of officer ▶ **Title ▶** **Date ▶**

See Parts II and III on back. Form **2553** (Rev. 12-90)

Form 2553 (Rev. 12-90) Page 2

Part II Selection of Fiscal Tax Year (All corporations using this Part must complete item O and one of items P, Q, or R.)

O Check the applicable box below to indicate whether the corporation is:

1. ☐ A new corporation adopting the tax year entered in item I, Part I.
2. ☐ An existing corporation retaining the tax year entered in item I, Part I.
3. ☐ An existing corporation changing to the tax year entered in item I, Part I.

P Complete item P if the corporation is using the expeditious approval provisions of Revenue Procedure 87-32, 1987-2 C.B. 396, to request: **(1)** a natural business year (as defined in section 4.01(1) of Rev. Proc. 87-32), or **(2)** a year that satisfies the ownership tax year test in section 4.01(2) of Rev. Proc. 87-32. Check the applicable box below to indicate the representation statement the corporation is making as required under section 4 of Rev. Proc. 87-32.

1. Natural Business Year ▶ ☐ I represent that the corporation is retaining or changing to a tax year that coincides with its natural business year as defined in section 4.01(1) of Rev. Proc. 87-32 and as verified by its satisfaction of the requirements of section 4.02(1) of Rev. Proc. 87-32. In addition, if the corporation is changing to a natural business year as defined in section 4.01(1), I further represent that such tax year results in less deferral of income to the owners than the corporation's present tax year. I also represent that the corporation is not described in section 3.01(2) of Rev. Proc. 87-32. (See instructions for additional information that must be attached.)

2. Ownership Tax Year ▶ ☐ I represent that shareholders holding more than half of the shares of the stock (as of the first day of the tax year to which the request relates) of the corporation have the same tax year or are concurrently changing to the tax year that the corporation adopts, retains, or changes to per item I, Part I. I also represent that the corporation is not described in section 3.01(2) of Rev. Proc. 87-32.

Note: *If you do not use item P and the corporation wants a fiscal tax year, complete either item Q or R below. Item Q is used to request a fiscal tax year based on a business purpose and to make a back-up section 444 election. Item R is used to make a regular section 444 election.*

Q Business Purpose—To request a fiscal tax year based on a business purpose, you must check box Q1 and pay a user fee. See instructions for details. You may also check box Q2 and/or box Q3.

1. Check here ▶ ☐ if the fiscal year entered in item I, Part I, is requested under the provisions of section 6.03 of Rev. Proc. 87-32. Attach to Form 2553 a statement showing the business purpose for the requested fiscal year. See instructions for additional information that must be attached.

2. Check here ▶ ☐ to show that the corporation intends to make a back-up section 444 election in the event the corporation's business purpose request is not approved by the IRS. (See instructions for more information.)

3. Check here ▶ ☐ to show that the corporation agrees to adopt or change to a tax year ending December 31 if necessary for the IRS to accept this election for S corporation status in the event: (1) the corporation's business purpose request is not approved and the corporation makes a back-up section 444 election, but is ultimately not qualified to make a section 444 election, or (2) the corporation's business purpose request is not approved and the corporation did not make a back-up section 444 election.

R Section 444 Election—To make a section 444 election, you must check box R1 and you may also check box R2.

1. Check here ▶ ☐ to show the corporation will make, if qualified, a section 444 election to have the fiscal tax year shown in item I, Part I. To make the election, you must complete **Form 8716,** Election To Have a Tax Year Other Than a Required Tax Year, and either attach it to Form 2553 or file it separately.

2. Check here ▶ ☐ to show that the corporation agrees to adopt or change to a tax year ending December 31 if necessary for the IRS to accept this election for S corporation status in the event the corporation is ultimately not qualified to make a section 444 election.

Part III Qualified Subchapter S Trust (QSST) Election Under Section 1361(d)(2)**

Income beneficiary's name and address	Social security number
Trust's name and address	Employer identification number

Date on which stock of the corporation was transferred to the trust (month, day, year) ▶

In order for the trust named above to be a QSST and thus a qualifying shareholder of the S corporation for which this Form 2553 is filed, I hereby make the election under section 1361(d)(2). Under penalties of perjury, I certify that the trust meets the definition requirements of section 1361(d)(3) and that all other information provided in Part III is true, correct, and complete.

Signature of income beneficiary or signature and title of legal representative or other qualified person making the election ——— Date

**Use of Part III to make the QSST election may be made only if stock of the corporation has been transferred to the trust on or before the date on which the corporation makes its election to be an S corporation. The QSST election must be made and filed separately if stock of the corporation is transferred to the trust after the date on which the corporation makes the S election.

APPENDIX II

GENERAL CORPORATION FORMS

Minutes

and

By Laws

of

INCORPORATED UNDER THE LAWS OF

WORKSHEETS

Instructions: Read the italicized directions, complete the blanks and check the appropriate boxes for your typists attention. Additional resolutions may be dictated or drafted on separate papers. Make an appropriate cross references in the margin of the worksheet where the italicized directions indicate. Additional pages should be numbered with the previous page number plus a letter suffix (5a, 5b, etc.)

ORGANIZATION MINUTES

☐ *prepare the organization meeting minutes, pages organization 1 through 7. Remove pages consent 1 and 2*

☐ *prepare organization consent minutes, pages consent 1 and 2, remove pages organization 1 through 7.*

MINUTES OF THE ORGANIZATION MEETING

ORGANIZATION 1
1. insert name of the corporation..................................
2. meeting held at..................................
3. date of meeting ....19 ....
4. time of meeting ....M.
5. following were present..................................
....
6. chairman of the meeting ....
7. secretary of the meeting ....
8. original Certificate of Incorporation filed on ....19..................

Organization 2 refers to assignments of subscribing stockholders (item 9) and resignations of directors (item 10). Typist should strike out unused paragraphs or remove entire page if both items 9 and 10 are unused.

ORGANIZATION 2
9. assignment of stock:

from	to	shares
....	....	....
....	....	....
....	....	....

10. resignations of..................................
....

organization 2a contains election of directors. If no election is to be held item 11 should be left blank and typist should remove organization 2a.

ORGANIZATION 2a
11. directors nominated..................................

ORGANIZATION 3
12. minutes and by-laws prepared by..................................
13. officers elected: president..................................
vice-president..................................
secretary..................................
treasurer..................................
....
14. impress seal in margin

ORGANIZATION 4
15. corporate offices established at
city of.................................. state of..................................
16. insert name of bank..................................
located at..................................

organization 5 contains blank space on which you may wish to add additional resolutions. Make an appropriate cross reference in this margin to the separate resolutions.

organization 5a contains resolutions adopting a proposal to exchange stock for property.
☐ *remove organization 5a*
☐ *complete item 17.*

ORGANIZATION 5a
17. proposal from ....
dated..................................19..................number of shares issued..................................

ORGANIZATION 6
18. dated..................................19..................

organization 6 contains a list of documents that may be appended to the minutes. Complete the documents checked below and strike out on the list those not checked.

☐ *Waiver of notice of meeting (see below for directions to complete)*
☐ *Certificate of incorporation*

worksheet 1

- ☐ *Assignments of subscriptions*
- ☐ *Resignations of directors*
- ☐ *Specimen stock certificates*
- ☐ *Resolution designating depository of funds*
- ☐ *Ratification of meeting*
- ☐ *By-laws (see below for directions to complete)*

WAIVER OF NOTICE OF THE ORGANIZATION MEETING

ORGANIZATION 7 1. insert name of the corporation..
2. insert: place of meeting..
date of meeting..19........
time of meeting....................M.
3. date the waiver..19........

CONSENT TO ACTION TAKEN IN LIEU OF ORGANIZATION MEETING

CONSENT 1 1. insert name of corporation..
2. certificate of incorporation filed on..19........
3. directors appointed..
....
4. officers appointed: president..
vice-president..
secretary..
treasurer..
....
5. minutes and by-laws prepared by..
6. impress seal in margin

If you wish to use a resolution adopting a proposal to exchange stock for property use the form on page organization 5a, renumber the page consent 1a and complete item 7.

7. proposal from..
dated..19........ number of shares issued..

Add additional resolutions on separate sheets numbered 1a, 1b, etc. Make an appropriate reference in this margin to the separate resolutions.

CONSENT 2 8. insert name of bank..
located at..
9. dated..19........

Consent 2 contains a list of documents that should be appended to the minutes.

BY-LAWS

ARTICLE

By-laws 1		insert name of corporation..
	I	office in the state of.. ....of..............................county of..
	II-1	annual meetings held on the..............day of..............................19........at.......M.
	II-2	special meetings called by the president at the request of not less than........................% of the shares entitled to vote.
By-laws 2	II-4	written notice of meeting shall be delivered not less than..............................days nor more than..............................days before the date of the meeting.
	II-5	directors may close transfer books for..............................days. To determine stockholders entitled to vote at a stockholders meeting directors may close books for..............................days. Directors may set record date..............................days in advance of determination of eligible stockholders. For purposes of stockholders meeting directors may set record date..............................days in advance.
By-laws 3	II-6	list of stockholders shall be made..............................days before meeting and kept on file..............................days.
	II-7	quorum of stockholders shall be..............................of the outstanding shares.
By-laws 5	III-2	number of directors shall be..
	III-5	notice of special meeting shall be given..............................days in advance.
By-laws 6	III-6	....directors shall constitute a quorum.
By-laws 11	VII	fiscal year shall begin on the..................day of..

worksheet 2

WAIVER OF NOTICE

OF THE ORGANIZATION MEETING

OF

We, the undersigned, being all the incorporators named in the certificate of incorporation of the above corporation hereby agree and consent that the organization meeting thereof be held on the date and at the time and place stated below and hereby waive all notice of such meeting and of any adjournment thereof.

Place of meeting

Date of meeting

Time of meeting

____

____

____

____

Dated:

organization 7

MINUTES OF

THE ORGANIZATION MEETING

OF

The organization meeting of incorporators was held at

on 19 at M.

The following were present

being all the incorporators of the corporation.

was appointed chairman of the meeting and was appointed secretary.

The secretary then presented and read to the meeting the waiver of notice of the meeting, subscribed by all the persons named in the certificate of incorporation, and it was ordered that it be appended to the minutes of the meeting.

The secretary then presented and read to the meeting a copy of the certificate of incorporation and reported that on 19 the original thereof was filed in the office of the Secretary of State of this State. The copy of the certificate of incorporation was ordered appended to the minutes of the meeting.

organization 1

The secretary then presented assignments executed by the subscribing stockholders as follows:

from	to	number of shares

RESOLVED, that the assignments of subscription rights as stated above are hereby approved and it is ordered that the assignments as executed by the subscribing stockholders be appended to the minutes of this meeting.

The secretary then presented to the meeting the resignation of

as directors of the corporation.

RESOLVED that the resignation of directors listed above is hereby approved and accepted and the form of resignation as executed by said directors be appended to these minutes.

The chairman then stated that nominations were in order for election of directors of the corporation to hold office until the first annual meeting of stockholders and until their successors shall be elected and shall qualify.

The following persons were nominated:

No further nominations being made nominations were closed and a vote was taken.

After the vote had been counted, the chairman declared that the foregoing named nominees were elected directors of the corporation.

The chairman then stated that the newly elected directors would assume their responsibilities immediately and that this meeting would be considered as the first meeting of directors to organize the corporation and to transact such business as should properly come before the meeting.

organization 2a

The secretary then presented a proposed form of by-laws prepared by

counsel to the corporation. The proposed by-laws were read to the meeting, considered and upon motion duly made, seconded and carried, were adopted as and for the by-laws of the corporation and ordered appended to the minutes of the meeting.

The chairman of the meeting then called for the election of officers of the corporation. The following persons were nominated to the office preceding their name:

president

vice-president

secretary

treasurer

No further nominations being made the nominations were closed and the directors proceeded to vote on the nominees. The chairman announced that the foregoing nominees were elected to the offices set before their respective names.

The secretary submitted to the meeting a seal proposed for use as the corporate seal, a specimen stock certificate proposed for use as the corporate certificate for stock, the corporate record book, and the stock transfer ledger. Upon motion duly made, seconded and carried, it was

RESOLVED, that the seal now presented at this meeting, an impression of which is directed to be made in the minutes of this meeting, be and the same hereby is adopted as the seal of the corporation, and further

RESOLVED, that the specimen stock certificate presented to this meeting be and hereby is adopted as the form of certificate of stock to be issued to represent shares in the corporation, and further

organization 3

RESOLVED, that the corporate record book, including the stock transfer ledger, be and hereby is adopted as the record book and stock transfer ledger of the corporation.

Upon motion duly made, seconded and carried, it was

RESOLVED, that the treasurer of the corporation be and hereby is authorized to pay all charges and expenses incident to or arising out of the organization of the corporation and to reimburse any person who has made any disbursement therefor.

Upon motion, duly made, seconded and carried, it was

RESOLVED, that an office of the corporation be established and maintained at
in the City of State of
and that meetings of the board of directors from time to time may be held either at the principal office or at such other place as the board of directors shall from time to time order.

Upon motion, duly made, seconded and carried, it was

RESOLVED, that for the purpose of authorizing the corporation to do business in any state, territory or dependency of the United States or any foreign country in which it is necessary or expedient for this corporation to transact business, the proper officers of this corporation are hereby authorized to appoint and substitute all necessary agents or attorneys for service of process, to designate and change the location of all necessary statutory offices and, under the corporate seal, to make and file all necessary certificates, reports, powers of attorney and other instruments as may be required by the laws of such state, territory, dependency or country to authorize the corporation to transact business therein.

The chairman then stated that it was desirable to designate a depository for the funds of the corporation. Thereupon, on motion duly made, seconded and unanimously adopted, it was

RESOLVED, that the treasurer be and hereby is authorized to open a bank account in behalf of the corporation with

located at
and a resolution for that purpose on the printed form of said bank was adopted and was ordered appended to the minutes of this meeting.

Upon motion duly made, seconded and carried, it was

RESOLVED, that the board of directors be and hereby is authorized to issue the unsubscribed capital stock of the corporation at such times and in such amounts as it shall determine, and to accept in payment thereof, cash, labor done, personal property, real property or leases thereof, or such other property as the board may deem necessary for the business of the corporation.

The secretary then presented to the meeting a written proposal from
dated 19 and addressed to this corporation.

Upon motion duly made, seconded and carried, the said proposal was ordered filed with the secretary, and he was requested to append a copy of the proposal to the minutes.

The proposal was taken up for consideration and the following resolution was on motion unanimously adopted

WHEREAS, a written proposal has been made to this corporation which proposal has been appended to these minutes, and

WHEREAS, in the judgment of the board of directors the assets proposed to be transferred to the corporation are reasonably worth the amount of the consideration demanded therefor, and that it is in the best interests of this corporation to accept the said offer as set forth in said proposal,

NOW THEREFORE, IT IS RESOLVED that said offer, as set forth in said proposal, be and the same hereby is approved and accepted, and that in accordance with the terms thereof, this corporation shall as full payment for said property issue to said offeror(s) or nominee(s) fully paid and non-assessable shares of this corporation, and it is

FURTHER RESOLVED, that upon the delivery to this corporation of said assets and the execution and delivery of such proper instruments as may be necessary to transfer and convey the same to this corporation, the officers of this corporation are authorized and directed to execute and deliver the certificate or certificates for such shares as are required to be issued and delivered on acceptance of said offer in accordance with the foregoing.

organization 5

Upon motion duly made, seconded and carried, it was

RESOLVED, that the corporation proceed to carry on the business for which it was incorporated, and further

RESOLVED, that the signing of these minutes shall constitute full ratification thereof and waiver of notice of the meeting by the signatories.

There being no further business before the meeting, on motion duly made, seconded and carried, the meeting was adjourned.

Dated:

____
chairman

____
secretary

A true copy of each of the following papers referred to in the foregoing minutes is appended hereto:

Waiver of notice of the meeting
Certificate of incorporation
Assignments of subscription
Resignation of directors
By-laws
Specimen stock certificates
Resolution designating depository of funds
Proposal

organization 6

ASSIGNMENT OF SUBSCRIPTION

KNOW ALL MEN BY THESE PRESENTS, that the undersigned in consideration of the sum of one dollar ($1.00) and other good and valuable consideration, receipt of which is hereby acknowledged, hereby sells, transfers and assigns unto

all his right, title and interest in and to the subscription for stock in

a corporation organized under the laws of the State of
and hereby authorizes, requests and directs said corporation to issue a certificate or certificates for the said shares in the name of and to
or such other person as he may order, upon payment by him of the amounts due on the said subscription and compliance with the other terms and conditions of said subscription.

IN WITNESS WHEREOF, I have hereunto set my hand and seal this day of 19

Witness: ______________________ ______________________

ASSIGNMENT OF SUBSCRIPTION

KNOW ALL MEN BY THESE PRESENTS, that the undersigned in consideration of the sum of one dollar ($1.00) and other good and valuable consideration, receipt of which is hereby acknowledged, hereby sells, transfers and assigns unto

all his right, title and interest in and to the subscription for stock in

a corporation organized under the laws of the State of
and hereby authorizes, requests and directs said corporation to issue a certificate or certificates for the said shares in the name of and to
or such other person as he may order, upon payment by him of the amounts due on the said subscription and compliance with the other terms and conditions of said subscription.

IN WITNESS WHEREOF, I have hereunto set my hand and seal this day of 19

Witness: ______________________ ______________________

ASSIGNMENT OF SUBSCRIPTION

KNOW ALL MEN BY THESE PRESENTS, that the undersigned in consideration of the sum of one dollar ($1.00) and other good and valuable consideration, receipt of which is hereby acknowledged, hereby sells, transfers and assigns unto

all his right, title and interest in and to the subscription for stock in

a corporation organized under the laws of the State of
and hereby authorizes, requests and directs said corporation to issue a certificate or certificates for the said shares in the name of and to
or such other person as he may order, upon payment by him of the amounts due on the said subscription and compliance with the other terms and conditions of said subscription.

IN WITNESS WHEREOF, I have hereunto set my hand and seal this day of 19

Witness: ______________________ ______________________

assignment

DIRECTORS' RESIGNATION

Gentlemen:

WE, THE UNDERSIGNED, hereby tender our resignations as directors of

to take effect immediately.

Dated:

Very truly yours,

____
Director

____
Director

____
Director

resignation

RATIFICATION OF ORGANIZATION MEETING

OF

We, the undersigned stockholders, having read the minutes of the organization meeting of the corporation held on 19 do hereby ratify, approve and confirm the actions taken and business transacted at said meeting as reported in the minutes of the meeting.

Dated:

stockholder

stockholder

stockholder

stockholder

ratification

CONSENT TO ACTION TAKEN IN LIEU OF ORGANIZATION MEETING

of

____

The undersigned being the incorporator(s) of the corporation hereby consent to and ratify the action taken to organize the corporation as hereafter stated:

The Certificate of Incorporation filed on
19 with the Secretary of State of this state was approved and inserted in the record book of the corporation.

The persons whose names appear below were appointed directors of the corporation to serve for a period of one year and until their successors are appointed or elected and shall qualify:

The persons whose names appear below were appointed officers of the corporation to serve for a period of one year and until their successors are appointed or elected and shall qualify:

President:
Vice-President:
Secretary:
Treasurer:

By-laws, regulating the conduct of the business and affairs of the corporation as prepared by

counsel for the corporation were adopted and inserted in the record book.

The seal, an impression of which appears in the margin of this consent was adopted as the corporate seal of the corporation, and the specimen of certificates for shares in the form exhibited and inserted in the record book was adopted as the corporate stock certificate.

consent 1

The directors were authorized to issue the unsubscribed capital stock of the corporation at such times and in such amounts as it shall determine, and to accept in payment thereof cash, labor done, personal property, real property or leases thereof, or such other property as the board may deem necessary for the business of the corporation.

The treasurer was authorized to open a bank account with

located at
and a resolution for that purpose on the printed form of said bank was adopted and inserted in the record book.

The president was authorized to designate the principal office of the corporation in this state as the office for service of process on the corporation, and to designate such further agents for service of process within or without this state as is in the best interests of the corporation. The president was further authorized to execute any and all certificates or documents to implement the above.

Dated

stockholder

stockholder

stockholder

A true copy of each of the following papers referred to in the foregoing consent is appended hereto.

Certificate of Incorporation
Specimen stock certificates
Resolution designating depository of funds
By-Laws

consent 2

BY-LAWS

OF

ARTICLE I - OFFICES

The principal office of the corporation in the State of shall be located in the of County of . The corporation may have such other offices, either within or without the State of incorporation as the board of directors may designate or as the business of the corporation may from time to time require.

ARTICLE II - STOCKHOLDERS

1. ANNUAL MEETING.

The annual meeting of the stockholders shall be held on the day of in each year, beginning with the year 19 at the hour o'clock M., for the purpose of electing directors and for the transaction of such other business as may come before the meeting. If the day fixed for the annual meeting shall be a legal holiday such meeting shall be held on the next succeeding business day.

2. SPECIAL MEETINGS.

Special meetings of the stockholders, for any purpose or purposes, unless otherwise prescribed by statute, may be called by the president or by the directors, and shall be called by the president at the request of the holders of not less than per cent of all the outstanding shares of the corporation entitled to vote at the meeting.

3. PLACE OF MEETING.

The directors may designate any place, either within or without the State unless otherwise prescribed by statute, as the place of meeting for any annual meeting or for any special meeting called by the directors. A waiver of notice signed by all stockholders entitled to vote at a meeting may designate

BY-LAWS (Continued)

any place, either within or without the state unless otherwise prescribed by statute, as the place for holding such meeting. If no designation is made, or if a special meeting be otherwise called, the place of meeting shall be the principal office of the corporation.

4. NOTICE OF MEETING.

Written or printed notice stating the place, day and and hour of the meeting and, in case of a special meeting, the purpose or purposes for which the meeting is called, shall be delivered not less than nor more than days before the date of the meeting, either personally or by mail, by or at the direction of the president, or the secretary, or the officer or persons calling the meeting, to each stockholder of record entitled to vote at such meeting. If mailed, such notice shall be deemed to be delivered when deposited in the United States mail, addressed to the stockholder at his address as it appears on the stock transfer books of the corporation, with postage thereon prepaid.

5. CLOSING OF TRANSFER BOOKS OR FIXING OF RECORD DATE.

For the purpose of determining stockholders entitled to notice of or to vote at any meeting of stockholders or any adjournment thereof, or stockholders entitled to receive payment of any dividend, or in order to make a determination of stockholders for any other proper purpose, the directors of the corporation may provide that the stock transfer books shall be closed for a stated period but not to exceed, in any case, days. If the stock transfer books shall be closed for the purpose of determining stockholders entitled to notice of or to vote at a meeting of stockholders, such books shall be closed for at least days immediately preceding such meeting. In lieu of closing the stock transfer books, the directors may fix in advance a date as the record date for any such determination of stockholders, such date in any case to be not more than days and, in case of a meeting of stockholders, not less than days prior to the date on which the particular action requiring such determination of stockholders is to be taken. If the stock transfer books are not closed and no record date is fixed for the determination of stockholders entitled to notice of or to vote at a meeting of stockholders, or stockholders entitled to receive payment of a dividend, the date on which notice of the meeting is mailed or the date on which the resolution of the directors declaring such dividend is adopted, as the case may be, shall be the record date for such determination of stockholders. When a determination of stockholders entitled to vote at any meeting of stockholders

BY-LAWS (Continued)

has been made as provided in this section, such determination shall apply to any adjournment thereof.

6. VOTING LISTS.

The officer or agent having charge of the stock transfer books for shares of the corporation shall make, at least   days before each meeting of stockholders, a complete list of the stockholders entitled to vote at such meeting, or any adjournment thereof, arranged in alphabetical order, with the address of and the number of shares held by each, which list, for a period of   days prior to such meeting, shall be kept on file at the principal office of the corporation and shall be subject to inspection by any stockholder at any time during usual business hours. Such list shall also be produced and kept open at the time and place of the meeting and shall be subject to the inspection of any stockholder during the whole time of the meeting. The original stock transfer book shall be prima facie evidence as to who are the stockholders entitled to examine such list or transfer books or to vote at the meeting of stockholders.

7. QUORUM.

At any meeting of stockholders   of the outstanding shares of the corporation entitled to vote, represented in person or by proxy, shall constitute a quorum at a meeting of stockholders. If less than said number of the outstanding shares are represented at a meeting, a majority of the shares so represented may adjourn the meeting from time to time without further notice. At such adjourned meeting at which a quorum shall be present or represented, any business may be transacted which might have been transacted at the meeting as originally notified. The stockholders present at a duly organized meeting may continue to transact business until adjournment, notwithstanding the withdrawal of enough stockholders to leave less than a quorum.

8. PROXIES.

At all meetings of stockholders, a stockholder may vote by proxy executed in writing by the stockholder or by his duly authorized attorney in fact. Such proxy shall be filed with the secretary of the corporation before or at the time of the meeting.

9. VOTING.

Each stockholder entitled to vote in accordance with the terms and provisions of the certificate of incorporation and these by-laws shall be entitled to one vote, in person or by

BY-LAWS (Continued)

proxy, for each share of stock entitled to vote held by such stockholders. Upon the demand of any stockholder, the vote for directors and upon any question before the meeting shall be by ballot. All elections for directors shall be decided by plurality vote; all other questions shall be decided by majority vote except as otherwise provided by the Certificate of Incorporation or the laws of this State.

10. ORDER OF BUSINESS.

The order of business at all meetings of the stockholders, shall be as follows:

1. Roll Call.
2. Proof of notice of meeting or waiver of notice.
3. Reading of minutes of preceding meeting.
4. Reports of Officers.
5. Reports of Committees.
6. Election of Directors.
7. Unfinished Business.
8. New Business.

11. INFORMAL ACTION BY STOCKHOLDERS.

Unless otherwise provided by law, any action required to be taken at a meeting of the shareholders, or any other action which may be taken at a meeting of the shareholders, may be taken without a meeting if a consent in writing, setting forth the action so taken, shall be signed by all of the shareholders entitled to vote with respect to the subject matter thereof.

BY-LAWS (Continued)

ARTICLE III - BOARD OF DIRECTORS

1. GENERAL POWERS.

The business and affairs of the corporation shall be managed by its board of directors. The directors shall in all cases act as a board, and they may adopt such rules and regulations for the conduct of their meetings and the management of the corporation, as they may deem proper, not inconsistent with these by-laws and the laws of this State.

2. NUMBER, TENURE AND QUALIFICATIONS.

The number of directors of the corporation shall be . Each director shall hold office until the next annual meeting of stockholders and until his successor shall have been elected and qualified.

3. REGULAR MEETINGS.

A regular meeting of the directors, shall be held without other notice than this by-law immediately after, and at the same place as, the annual meeting of stockholders. The directors may provide, by resolution, the time and place for the holding of additional regular meetings without other notice than such resolution.

4. SPECIAL MEETINGS.

Special meetings of the directors may be called by or at the request of the president or any two directors. The person or persons authorized to call special meetings of the directors may fix the place for holding any special meeting of the directors called by them.

5. NOTICE.

Notice of any special meeting shall be given at least days previously thereto by written notice delivered personally, or by telegram or mailed to each director at his business address. If mailed, such notice shall be deemed to be delivered when deposited in the United States mail so addressed, with postage thereon prepaid. If notice be given by telegram, such notice shall be deemed to be delivered when the telegram is delivered to the telegraph company. The attendance of a director at a meeting shall constitute a waiver of notice of such meeting, except where a director attends a meeting for the express purpose of objecting to the transaction of any business because the meeting is not lawfully called or convened.

By-Laws 5

BY-LAWS (Continued)

6. QUORUM.

At any meeting of the directors shall constitute a quorum for the transaction of business, but if less than said number is present at a meeting, a majority of the directors present may adjourn the meeting from time to time without further notice.

7. MANNER OF ACTING.

The act of the majority of the directors present at a meeting at which a quorum is present shall be the act of the directors.

8. NEWLY CREATED DIRECTORSHIPS AND VACANCIES.

Newly created directorships resulting from an increase in the number of directors and vacancies occurring in the board for any reason except the removal of directors without cause may be filled by a vote of a majority of the directors then in office, although less than a quorum exists. Vacancies occurring by reason of the removal of directors without cause shall be filled by vote of the stockholders. A director elected to fill a vacancy caused by resignation, death or removal shall be elected to hold office for the unexpired term of his predecessor.

9. REMOVAL OF DIRECTORS.

Any or all of the directors may be removed for cause by vote of the stockholders or by action of the board. Directors may be removed without cause only by vote of the stockholders.

10. RESIGNATION.

A director may resign at any time by giving written notice to the board, the president or the secretary of the corporation. Unless otherwise specified in the notice, the resignation shall take effect upon receipt thereof by the board or such officer, and the acceptance of the resignation shall not be necessary to make it effective.

11. COMPENSATION.

No compensation shall be paid to directors, as such, for their services, but by resolution of the board a fixed sum and expenses for actual attendance at each regular or special meeting of the board may be authorized. Nothing herein contained shall be construed to preclude any director from serving the corporation in any other capacity and receiving compensation therefor.

By-Laws 6

BY-LAWS (Continued)

12. PRESUMPTION OF ASSENT.

A director of the corporation who is present at a meeting of the directors at which action on any corporate matter is taken shall be presumed to have assented to the action taken unless his dissent shall be entered in the minutes of the meeting or unless he shall file his written dissent to such action with the person acting as the secretary of the meeting before the adjournment thereof or shall forward such dissent by registered mail to the secretary of the corporation immediately after the adjournment of the meeting. Such right to dissent shall not apply to a director who voted in favor of such action.

13. EXECUTIVE AND OTHER COMMITTEES.

The board, by resolution, may designate from among its members an executive committee and other committees, each consisting of three or more directors. Each such committee shall serve at the pleasure of the board.

BY-LAWS (Continued)

ARTICLE IV - OFFICERS

1. NUMBER.

The officers of the corporation shall be a president, a vice-president, a secretary and a treasurer, each of whom shall be elected by the directors. Such other officers and assistant officers as may be deemed necessary may be elected or appointed by the directors.

2. ELECTION AND TERM OF OFFICE.

The officers of the corporation to be elected by the directors shall be elected annually at the first meeting of the directors held after each annual meeting of the stockholders. Each officer shall hold office until his successor shall have been duly elected and shall have qualified or until his death or until he shall resign or shall have been removed in the manner hereinafter provided.

3. REMOVAL.

Any officer or agent elected or appointed by the directors may be removed by the directors whenever in their judgment the best interests of the corporation would be served thereby, but such removal shall be without prejudice to the contract rights, if any, of the person so removed.

4. VACANCIES.

A vacancy in any office because of death, resignation, removal, disqualification or otherwise, may be filled by the directors for the unexpired portion of the term.

5. PRESIDENT.

The president shall be the principal executive officer of the corporation and, subject to the control of the directors, shall in general supervise and control all of the business and affairs of the corporation. He shall, when present, preside at all meetings of the stockholders and of the directors. He may sign, with the secretary or any other proper officer of the corporation thereunto authorized by the directors, certificates for shares of the corporation, any deeds, mortgages, bonds, contracts, or other instruments which the directors have authorized to be executed, except in cases where the signing and execution thereof shall be expressly delegated by the directors or by these by-laws to some other officer or agent of the corporation, or shall be required by law to be otherwise signed or executed; and in general shall

BY-LAWS (Continued)

perform all duties incident to the office of president and such other duties as may be prescribed by the directors from time to time.

6. VICE-PRESIDENT.

In the absence of the president or in event of his death, inability or refusal to act, the vice-president shall perform the duties of the president, and when so acting, shall have all the powers of and be subject to all the restrictions upon the president. The vice-president shall perform such other duties as from time to time may be assigned to him by the President or by the directors.

7. SECRETARY.

The secretary shall keep the minutes of the stockholders' and of the directors' meetings in one or more books provided for that purpose, see that all notices are duly given in accordance with the provisions of these by-laws or as required, be custodian of the corporate records and of the seal of the corporation and keep a register of the post office address of each stockholder which shall be furnished to the secretary by such stockholder, have general charge of the stock transfer books of the corporation and in general perform all duties incident to the office of secretary and such other duties as from time to time may be assigned to him by the president or by the directors.

8. TREASURER.

If required by the directors, the treasurer shall give a bond for the faithful discharge of his duties in such sum and with such surety or sureties as the directors shall determine. He shall have charge and custody of and be responsible for all funds and securities of the corporation; receive and give receipts for moneys due and payable to the corporation from any source whatsoever, and deposit all such moneys in the name of the corporation in such banks, trust companies or other depositories as shall be selected in accordance with these by-laws and in general perform all of the duties incident to the office of treasurer and such other duties as from time to time may be assigned to him by the president or by the directors.

9. SALARIES.

The salaries of the officers shall be fixed from time to time by the directors and no officer shall be prevented from receiving such salary by reason of the fact that he is also a director of the corporation.

BY-LAWS (Continued)

ARTICLE V - CONTRACTS, LOANS, CHECKS AND DEPOSITS

1. CONTRACTS.

The directors may authorize any officer or officers, agent or agents, to enter into any contract or execute and deliver any instrument in the name of and on behalf of the corporation, and such authority may be general or confined to specific instances.

2. LOANS.

No loans shall be contracted on behalf of the corporation and no evidences of indebtedness shall be issued in its name unless authorized by a resolution of the directors. Such authority may be general or confined to specific instances.

3. CHECKS, DRAFTS, ETC.

All checks, drafts or other orders for the payment of money, notes or other evidences of indebtedness issued in the name of the corporation, shall be signed by such officer or officers, agent or agents of the corporation and in such manner as shall from time to time be determined by resolution of the directors.

4. DEPOSITS.

All funds of the corporation not otherwise employed shall be deposited from time to time to the credit of the corporation in such banks, trust companies or other depositaries as the directors may select.

ARTICLE VI - CERTIFICATES FOR SHARES AND THEIR TRANSFER

1. CERTIFICATES FOR SHARES.

Certificates representing shares of the corporation shall be in such form as shall be determined by the directors. Such certificates shall be signed by the president and by the secretary or by such other officers authorized by law and by the directors. All certificates for shares shall be consecutively numbered or otherwise identified. The name and address of the stockholders, the number of shares and date of issue, shall be entered on the stock transfer books of the corporation. All certificates surrendered to the corporation for transfer shall be canceled and no new certificate shall be issued until the

BY-LAWS (Continued)

former certificate for a like number of shares shall have been surrendered and canceled, except that in case of a lost, destroyed or mutilated certificate a new one may be issued therefor upon such terms and indemnity to the corporation as the directors may prescribe.

2. TRANSFERS OF SHARES.

(a) Upon surrender to the corporation or the transfer agent of the corporation of a certificate for shares duly endorsed or accompanied by proper evidence of succession, assignment or authority to transfer, it shall be the duty of the corporation to issue a new certificate to the person entitled thereto, and cancel the old certificate; every such transfer shall be entered on the transfer book of the corporation which shall be kept at its principal office.

(b) The corporation shall be entitled to treat the holder of record of any share as the holder in fact thereof, and, accordingly, shall not be bound to recognize any equitable or other claim to or interest in such share on the part of any other person whether or not it shall have express or other notice thereof, except as expressly provided by the laws of this state.

ARTICLE VII - FISCAL YEAR

The fiscal year of the corporation shall begin on the day of in each year.

ARTICLE VIII - DIVIDENDS

The directors may from time to time declare, and the corporation may pay, dividends on its outstanding shares in the manner and upon the terms and conditions provided by law.

ARTICLE IX - SEAL

The directors shall provide a corporate seal which shall be circular in form and shall have inscribed thereon the name of the corporation, the state of incorporation, year of incorporation and the words, ''Corporate Seal''.

BY-LAWS (Continued)

ARTICLE X - WAIVER OF NOTICE

Unless otherwise provided by law, whenever any notice is required to be given to any stockholder or director of the corporation under the provisions of these by-laws or under the provisions of the articles of incorporation, a waiver thereof in writing, signed by the person or persons entitled to such notice, whether before or after the time stated therein, shall be deemed equivalent to the giving of such notice.

ARTICLE XI - AMENDMENTS

These by-laws may be altered, amended or repealed and new by-laws may be adopted by a vote of the stockholders representing a majority of all the shares issued and outstanding, at any annual stockholders' meeting or at any special stockholders' meeting when the proposed amendment has been set out in the notice of such meeting.

By-Laws 12

NOTICE OF ANNUAL MEETING OF STOCKHOLDERS

of

____

PLEASE TAKE NOTICE THAT the annual meeting of shareholders of the corporation for the purpose of electing directors and the transaction of such other business as may properly come before the meeting will be held on the date and at the time and place stated below.

Date of meeting
Time of meeting
Place of meeting

The share transfer ledger of the corporation shall remain closed from 19 to 19

Dated

____
secretary

AFFIDAVIT OF MAILING OF
NOTICE OF ANNUAL MEETING OF SHAREHOLDERS

STATE OF
COUNTY OF ss.:

being duly sworn according to law deposes and says:

I am the secretary of that on 19 I personally deposited in a post office box in the city of county of state of copies of the above notice of annual meeting of shareholders, each enclosed in a securely sealed postage paid envelope, one of the notices addressed to each person whose name appears on the annexed list of shareholders and to their respective post office addresses as therein set forth.

Sworn to before me this
day of 19

____
secretary

____

SM 4a

WAIVER OF NOTICE OF THE ANNUAL MEETING OF STOCKHOLDERS

____

We, the undersigned shareholders, hereby agree and consent that the annual meeting of shareholders of the corporation be held on the date and at the time and place stated below for the purpose of electing directors of the corporation and the transaction thereat of all such other business as may lawfully come before said meeting and hereby waive all notice of the meeting and any adjournment thereof.

Date of meeting

Time of meeting

Place of meeting

Dated

____

____

____

____

SM 4

MINUTES OF THE ANNUAL MEETING OF STOCKHOLDERS

of

____

The annual meeting of the stockholders of the corporation was held at

on 19 at M.

The meeting was called to order by the of the corporation.

The secretary then reported that the meeting had been called pursuant to a notice of meeting and/or waiver of notice thereof in accordance with the by-laws. It was ordered that a copy of the notice and waiver of notice be appended to the minutes of the meeting.

The secretary then read the roll of stockholders from the stock transfer ledger. The following stockholders were present in person or by proxy:

Stockholder	Shares	In Person	By Proxy

The chairman stated that a majority of the total number of shares issued and outstanding was represented and that the meeting was complete and ready to transact any business before it. It was ordered that proxies be appended to the minutes of the meeting.

SM 1

STOCKHOLDER MINUTES (Continued)

The president then gave a general report of the business and finances of the corporation and the secretary reported the following changes of stockholders since the last such report:

The chairman then stated that the election of directors of the corporation was now in order. The following were nominated as directors:

The chairman appointed
and as Inspectors of Election and they subscribed and verified their oath of office. The oaths of the Inspectors were appended to the minutes of the meeting. A ballot was taken, the vote was canvassed and the Inspectors of Election reported the following votes cast for directors of the corporation.

Nominee	Number of Votes

The chairman declared the following nominees duly elected directors of the corporation to serve until the next annual meeting of stockholders or until their successors are elected and shall qualify:

The following action was taken at the meeting:

SM 2

STOCKHOLDER MINUTES (Continued)

There being no further business, the meeting was, on motion, adjourned.

Dated

____
secretary

INSPECTORS REPORT

We the undersigned Inspectors of Election, having faithfully and impartially conducted the election of directors, did receive the votes of the shareholders as set forth in these minutes.

Dated

____
Inspector of Election

____
Inspector of Election

RATIFICATION

We, the undersigned shareholders, or assignees thereof, have read these minutes and do hereby approve, ratify and confirm all business transacted as reported herein.

____

____

____

____

The following have been appended to the minutes:

Waiver of Notice
Notice of Meeting and Affidavit of Mailing
Proxy(ies)
Oath of Inspectors of Election

SM 3

PROXY FOR ANNUAL MEETING OF SHAREHOLDERS

of

____

KNOW ALL MEN BY THESE PRESENTS, that I am the owner of

and I hereby appoint and constitute

my true and lawful attorney and proxy with full power of substitution and revocation, to attend and represent me at the annual meeting of shareholders of the corporation to be held on 19 and for and on my behalf to vote on any question, proposition or resolution, or any other matter which may come before the meeting or any adjournment thereof upon which I would be entitled to vote if personally present.

This proxy shall be void if I personally attend the said meeting.

IN WITNESS WHEREOF, I have executed this proxy on the day of 19

____

SM 5a

OATH OF INSPECTORS OF ELECTION

of

____

STATE OF
COUNTY OF ss.:

We, the undersigned, being duly sworn, each for himself deposes and says that he will faithfully, truly and honestly perform the duties of Inspector of Election of the election of directors of the corporation to be held at the annual meeting of shareholders of the corporation on 19 with strict impartiality and according to the best of his ability, understanding and judgment.

____
Inspector of Election

____
Inspector of Election

Severally sworn to before me this
day of 19

____

SM 5

WAIVER OF NOTICE OF THE REGULAR MEETING OF DIRECTORS

of

____

We, the undersigned, being all the directors of the corporation hereby agree and consent that the regular meeting of directors of the corporation be held on the date and the time and at the place stated below for the purpose of transacting any and all business that should properly come before the meeting and hereby waive all notice of the meeting and of any adjournment thereof.

Date of meeting

Time of meeting

Place of meeting

Dated

____
director

____
director

____
director

DM 3

MINUTES OF THE REGULAR MEETING OF DIRECTORS

of

____

The regular meeting of directors of the corporation was held at

on 19 at M.

The following were present

being a quorum and all of the directors of the corporation.

was elected chairman of the meeting and was appointed secretary thereof.

The secretary then presented and read to the meeting a waiver of notice of meeting, subscribed by all the directors of the corporation, and it was ordered that it be appended to the minutes of the meeting.

The minutes of the preceeding meeting of the board of directors held on 19 was thereupon read and adopted.

The president then rendered a general report of the business of the corporation, the secretary presented his report and the treasurer rendered a report of the finances of the corporation. The officers' reports were received and ordered on file.

The following were duly nominated and a vote having been taken were unanimously elected officers of the corporation to serve for one year and until their successors are elected and shall qualify:

President

Vice-President

Secretary

Treasurer

There being no further business before the meeting, on motion duly made, seconded and carried, the meeting adjourned.

Dated

____
secretary

____
chairman

The following have been appended to these minutes:

Waiver of Notice

WAIVER OF NOTICE OF SPECIAL MEETING OF DIRECTORS

of

____

We, the undersigned being all the directors of the corporation hereby agree and consent that the special meeting of directors be held at the date, time and place stated below and for the purposes stated below and the transaction thereat of all such other business as may lawfully come before the meeting and hereby waive all notice of the meeting and any adjournment thereof.

Date of meeting

Time of meeting

Place of meeting

Purpose of meeting

Dated

____
director

____
director

____
director

SDM 3

MINUTES OF THE SPECIAL MEETING OF DIRECTORS

of

____

The special meeting of directors of the corporation was held at

on 19 at M.

The following directors were present:

being all the directors of the corporation and a quorum.

was elected chairman of the meeting and was elected secretary of the meeting.

The secretary then presented and read a waiver of notice of the meeting, subscribed by all the directors of the corporation, and it was ordered that it be appended to the minutes of the meeting.

The chairman then stated that the meeting was called for the purpose of

There being no further business before the meeting, on motion duly made, seconded and carried, the meeting adjourned.

Dated

____
chairman

____
secretary

The following have been appended to the minutes of the meeting:

Waiver of Notice

SDM 1

MINUTES OF SPECIAL MEETING OF DIRECTORS

OF

A special meeting of the Board of Directors of the Corporation was held at the time, date and place set forth below.

All of the Directors being present, the meeting was called to order by the Chairman. The Chairman advised that all the shareholders had executed written consents to the election by the Corporation to be treated as a "small business corporation". Upon motion duly made, seconded and unanimously carried, it was

RESOLVED, that the proper officers of the corporation are hereby authorized to take any and all action necessary to comply with the requirements of the Internal Revenue Service for making an election pursuant to Sub Chapter S of the Internal Revenue Code, Sec. 1362, and it was further

RESOLVED, that the signing of these minutes by the Directors shall constitute full ratification thereof and waiver of notice of the meeting by the signatories.

There being no further business to come before the meeting, upon motion duly made, seconded and unanimously carried, the meeting was adjourned.

Place:
Date:
Time:

____
Secretary

____
Chairman

____
Director

____
Director

____
Director

MINUTES OF SPECIAL MEETING OF DIRECTORS

OF

A special meeting of the Board of Directors of the Corporation was held on 19 at M. at

All of the Directors being present, the meeting was called to order by the Chairman. The Chairman advised that the meeting was called to approve and adopt a medical care expense reimbursement plan. A copy of the plan was presented to those present and upon motion duly made, seconded and unanimously carried, it was

RESOLVED, that the "Medical Care Reimbursement Plan" presented to the meeting is hereby approved and adopted, that a copy of the plan shall be appended to these minutes, and that the proper officers of the corporation are hereby authorized to take whatever action is necessary to implement the plan, and it is further

RESOLVED, that the signing of these minutes by the Directors shall constitute full ratification thereof and waiver of notice of the meeting by the signatories.

There being no further business to come before the meeting, upon motion duly made, seconded and unanimously carried, the meeting was adjourned.

Secretary

Chairman

Director

Director

Director

CORPORATE RECORD TICKLER

corporate name .... annual meeting date .... fiscal year ends ....

attention .... address .... zip .... telephone ....

attorney in charge .... related corporations ....

accountants .... accountant in charge ....

address .... zip .... telephone ....

registered agent .... address .... zip .... telephone ....

principal shareholders ....

	19...........	19...........	19...........
Chairperson			
Director			
Director			
Director			
President			
Vice Pres.			
Secretary			
Treasurer			

PROCEEDINGS: (check box if minutes completed)

Type Key: Annual Meeting Shareholder — AMS, Annual Meeting Directors — AMD, Special Meeting Shareholders — SMS, Special Meeting Directors — SMD, Action Taken Without Meeting, Shareholders — ATS, Action Taken Without Meeting, Directors — ATD, Committee Meeting — CM.

Date	Type		Date	Type		Date	Type	
		☐			☐			☐
		☐			☐			☐
		☐			☐			☐
		☐			☐			☐
		☐			☐			☐

LOCATOR: Corporate records sent to:

Corporate records sent to	date	date returned

☐ Extra seal in client's office.

INSTRUCTIONS

Maintain a separate binder with these control forms for each corporation represented by the firm. Organize it alphabetically or by date of the annual meeting or fiscal year end. The date method provides a convenient tickler for an annual review. Additional sheets and control binder available from the publisher. Prior to tax audit you can now easily determine if minutes are up to date.

Blumbergs Law Products T 5102—Corporate record tickler. 7-90

MEDICAL CARE REIMBURSEMENT PLAN OF

1. BENEFITS

The Corporation shall reimburse all eligible employees for expenses incurred by themselves and their dependents, as defined in IRC §152, as amended, for medical care, as defined in IRC §213(e), as amended, subject to the conditions and limitations as hereinafter set forth. It is the intention of the Corporation that the benefits payable to eligible employees hereunder shall be excluded from their gross income pursuant to IRC §105, as amended.

2. ELIGIBILITY

3. LIMITATIONS

(a) The Corporation shall reimburse any eligible employee no more than $ in any fiscal year for medical care expenses.

(b) Reimbursement or payment provided under this Plan shall be made by the Corporation only in the event and to the extent that such reimbursement or payment is not provided under any insurance policy(ies), whether owned by the Corporation or the employee, or under any other health and accident or wage continuation plan. In the event that there is such an insurance policy or plan in effect, providing for reimbursement in whole or in part, then to the extent of the coverage under such policy or plan, the Corporation shall be relieved of any and all liability hereunder.

4. SUBMISSION OF PROOF

Any eligible employee applying for reimbursement under this Plan shall submit to the Corporation, at least quarterly, all bills for medical care, including premium notices for accident or health insurance, for verification by the Corporation prior to payment. Failure to comply herewith, may at the discretion of the Corporation, terminate such eligible employee's right to said reimbursement.

5. DISCONTINUATION

This Plan shall be subject to termination at any time by vote of the board of directors of the Corporation; provided, however, that medical care expenses incurred prior to such termination shall be reimbursed or paid in accordance with the terms of this Plan.

6. DETERMINATION

The president shall determine all questions arising from the administration and interpretation of the Plan except where reimbursement is claimed by the president. In such case determination shall be made by the board of directors.

Adopted by the Board of Directors
on 19

....
Secretary

T 1221—Trade Name Certificate. JULIUS BLUMBERG, INC., LAW BLANK PUBLISHERS

Know all Men by these Presents,

The undersigned do hereby certify that h own conduct and transact the business of

under the assumed name of

and that the Post Office address of said business is

and that there are no other persons associated with the undersigned in the conduct of said business; and that the post office addresses given below are correct.

IN WITNESS WHEREOF, have hereunto set hand at

this day of 19

Name...

Address...

Name...

Address...

Name...

Address...

Name...

Address...

Name...

Address...

STATE OF CONNECTICUT
COUNTY OF } *ss.:*

On this the day of 19 , before me, the undersigned officer, personally appeared

known to me (or satisfactorily proven) to be the person whose name subscribed to the within instrument and acknowledged that he executed the same for the purposes therein contained.

In witness whereof I hereunto set my hand.

....

....
Title of Officer

The above and foregoing is a true copy of the original certificate on file in the office of the Town Clerk of the Town of

Attest:

.... *Town Clerk*

Certificate of Incorporation of

under Section 402 of the Business Corporation Law

IT IS HEREBY CERTIFIED THAT:

(1) The name of the proposed corporation is

(2) The purpose or purposes for which this corporation is formed, are as follows, to wit:
To engage in any lawful act or activity for which corporations may be organized under the Business Corporation Law. The corporation is not formed to engage in any act or activity requiring the consent or approval of any state official, department, board, agency or other body.*

The corporation, in furtherance of its corporate purposes above set forth, shall have all of the powers enumerated in Section 202 of the Business Corporation Law, subject to any limitations provided in the Business Corporation Law or any other statute of the State of New York.

*If specific consent or approval is required delete this paragraph, insert specific purposes and obtain consent or approval prior to filing.

(3) The office of the corporation is to be located in the County of
State of New York.

(4) The aggregate number of shares which the corporation shall have the authority to issue is

(5) The Secretary of State is designated as agent of the corporation upon whom process against it may be served. The post office address to which the Secretary of State shall mail a copy of any process against the corporation served upon him is

(6) A director of the corporation shall not be liable to the corporation or its shareholders for damages for any breach of duty in such capacity except for

(i) liability if a judgment or other final adjudication adverse to a director establishes that his or her acts or omissions were in bad faith or involved intentional misconduct or a knowing violation of law or that the director personally gained in fact a financial profit or other advantage to which he or she was not legally entitled or that the director's acts violated BCL § 719, or

(ii) liability for any act or omission prior to the adoption of this provision.

The undersigned incorporator, or each of them if there are more than one, is of the age of eighteen years or over.

IN WITNESS WHEREOF, this certificate has been subscribed on 19 by the undersigned who affirm(s) that the statements made herein are true under the penalties of perjury.

Type name of incorporator — Signature

Address

Type name of incorporator — Signature

Address

Type name of incorporator — Signature

Address

Certificate of Incorporation of

under Article 15 of the Business Corporation Law

IT IS HEREBY CERTIFIED THAT:

(1) The name of the proposed corporation is

(2) The purpose for which the corporation is formed is to practice the profession of

The corporation, in furtherance of its corporate purposes set forth above, shall have all of the powers conferred by the Business Corporation Law upon corporations formed thereunder, subject to any limitations contained in Article 15 of the Business Corporation Law or in accordance with any other provisions of any other statute of the State of New York.

(3) The name, residence address, profession, professional license or certificate number and office to be held of all individuals who are to be the original shareholders, directors and officers of the corporation, are as follows:

Attached hereto is a certificate or certificates issued by the licensing authority certifying that each of the proposed shareholders, directors and officers is authorized by law to practice the profession which the corporation is being organized to practice.

CERTIFICATE OF INCORPORATION (Continued)

(4) The office of the corporation is to be located in the county of
State of New York.

(5) The aggregate number of shares which the corporation is authorized to issue is

(6) The Secretary of State is designated as the agent of the corporation upon whom process against it may be served. The post office address to which the Secretary of State shall mail a copy of any process against the corporation served upon him is

IN WITNESS WHEREOF, *the undersigned incorporator(s), being 18 years of age, subscribe this certificate and affirm(s) that the statements made herein are true under the penalties of perjury.*

Dated

....
Type Name Signature

....
Address

....
Type Name Signature

....
Address

....
Type Name Signature

....
Address

M 385— Certificate of Amendment of Certificate of Incorporation: Business Corporation Law §805: 12-85.

Certificate of Amendment of the Certificate of Incorporation of

under Section 805 of the Business Corporation Law

IT IS HEREBY CERTIFIED THAT:

(1) The name of the corporation is

(2) The certificate of incorporation was filed by the department of state on the day of 19 .

*(3) The certificate of incorporation of this corporation is hereby amended to effect the following change**

**Set forth the subject matter of each provision of the certificate of incorporation which is to be amended or eliminated and the full text of the provision(s), if any, which are to be substituted or added. If an amendment provides for a change of issued shares, the number and kind of shares changed, the number and kind of shares resulting from such change and the terms of change. If an amendment makes two or more such changes, a like statement shall be included in respect to each change.*

(4) The amendment to the certificate of incorporation was authorized:

- ** first, by vote of the board of directors.*
- ** first, by unanimous written consent of all the directors.*
- ** and then at a meeting of shareholders by vote of a majority of all the outstanding shares entitled to vote thereon.*
- ** and then by unanimous written consent of the holders of all the outstanding shares entitled to vote thereon.*
- ** and then at a meeting of shareholders by vote of of all the outstanding shares entitled to vote thereon as required by the certificate of incorporation.*

*STRIKE OUT WHERE INAPPLICABLE

IN WITNESS WHEREOF, *this certificate has been subscribed this day of 19 by the undersigned who affirm(s) that the statements made herein are true under the penalties of perjury.*

Type name	*Capacity in which signed*	*Signature*
....	....	....
....	....	....
....	....	....

Certificate of Incorporation of

under the New Jersey Business Corporation Act

IT IS HEREBY CERTIFIED THAT:

(1) The name of the proposed corporation is

(2) The corporation may engage in any activity within the purposes for which corporations may be organized under the New Jersey Business Corporation Act.*

* Specific purposes may be set forth but are not required.

(3) The aggregate number of shares which the corporation shall have the authority to issue is

(4) The address of the corporation's initial office is

(5) The name of the corporation's initial registered agent at such address is

(6) The number of directors constituting the first board is

(7) The name and address of each person who is to serve as such director is

Name	Address

(8) A director shall not be personally liable to the corporation or its shareholders for damages for breach of any duty owed to the corporation or its shareholders, except for liability for any breach of duty based upon an act or omission (a) in breach of such director's duty of loyalty to the corporation or its shareholders, (b) not in good faith or involving a knowing violation of law, or (c) resulting in receipt by such director of an improper personal benefit.

The undersigned incorporator, or each of them if there are more than one, is of the age of eighteen years or over.

IN WITNESS WHEREOF, this certificate has been subscribed this day of 19 by the undersigned.

Type name of incorporator — Signature of incorporator

Address

Type name of incorporator — Signature of incorporator

Address

Type name of incorporator — Signature of incorporator

Address

CERTIFICATE OF AMENDMENT (Continued)

DEPARTMENT OF STATE, BUREAU OF CORPORATIONS
162 Washington Ave., Albany, N. Y. 12231

Re: ....
Corporate name

....
Assumed name

Please file the enclosed Certificate of Amendment of Assumed Name for the above corporation. Fees[1] for filing of $.................. are enclosed.

☐ *Please forward* .... *certified copy(ies) of the original certificate. Fees[2] of $* .... *for certified copy(ies) are enclosed.*

Our[2] .... check for $.................. to cover the cost of filing *and the certified copy(ies)* is enclosed. Send the receipt(s) *and certified copy(ies)* to..

....

.... Print or type name   .... Signature

1 See "FEES" section of form for amount of filing fees.   2 See reverse side for certified copy fees and method payment.

Separate at perforation before mailing.

New York State
DEPARTMENT OF STATE
CORPORATIONS AND STATE RECORDS DIVISION
162 Washington Avenue
Albany, NY 12231

CORPORATION—CERTIFICATE OF AMENDMENT OF ASSUMED NAME
(Pursuant to Section 130 General Business Law)

FEES: THE FILING FEE PAYABLE TO THE SECRETARY OF STATE IS $25.00. IF THE AMENDMENT IS FOR CORPORATE NAME CHANGE OR PRINCIPAL PLACE OF BUSINESS ADDRESS CHANGE, ADD $25.00 FOR EACH COUNTY THAT WAS PREVIOUSLY LISTED IN WHICH BUSINESS IS CONDUCTED UNDER ASSUMED NAME. IF THE AMENDMENT AFFECTS CERTAIN COUNTIES ONLY, ADD $25.00 FOR EACH COUNTY AFFECTED BY THE AMENDMENT.

1. Present corporation name ....
2. If corporation name different on last assumed name certificate or amendment, state name previously listed. ....
3. Assumed name..
4. The date original Certificate of Assumed Name was filed..
5. The date, if any, the last Certificate of Amendment of Assumed Name was filed ....
6. The following changes are being made. Check appropriate box(es).
   A. ☐ Corporate name, as indicated above.
   B. ☐ Assumed name.
   C. ☐ Principal place of business. (Enter change in Item 8, below.)
   D. ☐ Counties, added or deleted, in which business is conducted under an assumed name. (Enter in Item 9, below.)
   E. ☐ Address(es) of specific business location(s) being added or deleted. (Enter in Item 10 below.)
7. The assumed name of the corporation is changed to:..
8. If principal place of business is being changed, state new address.
   .... No. and Street
   .... City State Zip Code County
9. Counties added .... Counties deleted..
   (If additional space needed, use reverse side.)
10. Specific business address(es) change. (If additional space needed, use reverse side.)
    Addition Deletion
    .... No. and Street .... No. and Street
    .... City Zip Code County .... City Zip Code County

Corporation officer signature..
Type name and office..

ACKNOWLEDGMENT (Must be completed)

State of.................................. County of.................................. ss.:

On.................................. 19.......... before me personally came ....
to me known, who being by me duly sworn, did depose and say that he/she is the ....
of.., the corporation described in the foregoing certificate, and acknowledged that he/she executed the same by order of the Board of Directors of such corporation.

....

Filer's address.. | For Department of state use only — Date filed..

Filer's address..
No. and Street City State Zip Code

CERTIFICATE OF AMENDMENT (Continued)

GBL § 130(4): A certified copy of the original certificate, or if an amended certificate has been filed, then of the most recent amended certificate filed shall be conspicuously displayed on the premises at each place in which the business for which the same was filed is conducted.

CERTIFIED COPY FEES: $10.00 for each certified copy.

PAYMENT: Certified check, money order or bank check. An attorney's check will be accepted up to $250. You may use one check to cover filing fees and certified copy fees.

Separate at perforation before mailing.

9. Counties added (cont'd) | Counties deleted (cont'd)

10. Business locations to be added (cont'd) | Business locations to be deleted (cont'd)

Added		Deleted	
No. and Street		No. and Street	
City	State	City	State
Zip Code	County	Zip Code	County
No. and Street		No. and Street	
City	State	City	State
Zip Code	County	Zip Code	County
No. and Street		No. and Street	
City	State	City	State
Zip Code	County	Zip Code	County
No. and Street		No. and Street	
City	State	City	State
Zip Code	County	Zip Code	County

Use continuation sheet if necessary

Do not use space below.

T 638—Certificate of discontinuance of assumed name by corporation 8 84

Blumbergs Law Products

JULIUS BLUMBERG, INC., PUBLISHER, NYC 10013

New York State
DEPARTMENT OF STATE
CORPORATIONS AND STATE RECORDS DIVISION
162 Washington Avenue
Albany, NY 12231

CORPORATION—CERTIFICATE OF DISCONTINUANCE OF ASSUMED NAME
(Pursuant to Section 130 General Business Law)

FEES: THE FILING FEE PAYABLE TO THE SECRETARY OF STATE IS $25.00.

1. Present corporation name....................

2. If corporation name different on last assumed name certificate or amendment, state name previously listed.
....

3. Principal place of business in New York State* ....
No. and Street
....
City State Zip Code County

* ☐ If none, check box and insert principal out-of-state address above.

4. Assumed name....................

5. The date the original Certificate of Assumed Name was filed....................

6. The date, if any, the last Certificate of Amendment of Assumed Name was filed....................

7. The reason for the discontinuance of the use of assumed name....................
....
....
....
....
....
....
....

Corporation officer signature....................
Type name and office....................

SAMPLE

ACKNOWLEDGMENT (Must be completed)

State of.................... County of....................ss.:
On.................... 19.......... before me personally came ....
to me known, who being by me duly sworn, did depose and say that he/she is the ....
of...................., the corporation described in the foregoing certificate, and acknowledged that he/she executed the same by order of the Board of Directors of such corporation.

....

Filer's name....................

For Department of State use only
Date filed....................

Filer's address....................
No. and Street City State Zip Code

CANCELLATION OF BUSINESS NAMES

868—Cancellation of Business Name   JULIUS BLUMBERG, INC., LAW BLANK PUBLISHERS

State of New Jersey }
County of } ss.:

I, (we)

do hereby certify that *(was) (were)* *conducting or transacting business under the name of*

at *in the*
County of *and having filed a certificate in the office of the County*
Clerk, County of *on the* *day of*
19 *, which certificate is still on record and I (we) now desire herewith*
to have the same cancelled and discharged of record.

NAMES	*RESIDENCE*	*P.O. ADDRESS*

In Witness Whereof, *have this* *day of* *19* *, made*
and signed this certificate.

....

....

....

....

State of New Jersey }
County of } ss.:

The undersigned being duly sworn according
to law on *oath* *depose* *and say* *that* *person* *named in the*
foregoing certificate and that the statements contained therein are true.

Sworn and subscribed to this
day of
A. D. 19
before me at

CERTIFICATE OF DIRECTORS' RESOLUTION

T 469—Standard N.Y.B.T.U. Form 8052:
Certificate of Directors' Resolution to Mortgage Corporate Property.

JULIUS BLUMBERG, INC., LAW BLANK PUBLISHERS

CONSULT YOUR LAWYER BEFORE SIGNING THIS INSTRUMENT—THIS INSTRUMENT SHOULD BE USED BY LAWYERS ONLY.

The undersigned, the secretary of

a New York corporation,

DOES HEREBY CERTIFY:

1. At a meeting of the board of directors of the above mentioned corporation, duly called and held this day at which a quorum was present and acted throughout, the board of directors unanimously adopted the following resolution, which has not been modified or rescinded:

RESOLVED, that the corporation execute and deliver to

or to any other person or corporation a mortgage covering the property owned by said corporation located at

such mortgage to be for the sum of $ to secure payment of a note of the corporation, bearing even date therewith, conditioned for the payment of said sum, with interest thereon,

that said note and mortgage
be in such form and contain such interest rate or rates, time of payment, including installment payments, and such other terms, provisions, conditions, stipulations and agreements as the officer of the corporation executing the same may deem proper and advisable; and that the president or vice president or any other officer of the corporation be and each of them hereby is authorized to execute and deliver such note and mortgage and such other instruments as such officer may deem proper and advisable and to affix the seal of the corporation thereto.

2. Neither the certificate of incorporation nor the by-laws contain any special requirement as to the number of directors required to pass such resolution.

3. The certificate of incorporation of the corporation does not require any vote or consent of shareholders to authorize the making of such mortgage.

This certificate is made and delivered in order to induce the lender referred to in the foregoing resolution to make the loan and accept the mortgage referred to therein and to induce any title insurance company to issue a policy of title insurance insuring to such lender the validity and priority of such mortgage.

IN WITNESS WHEREOF, the undersigned has hereto affixed h hand and the seal of the above mentioned corporation this day of 19

....

(Corporate Seal)

STATE OF NEW YORK, COUNTY OF ss.:

On the day of 19 , before me came
to me known and known to me to be the individual described in and who executed the foregoing certificate and acknowledged to me that he executed the same.

....
Notary Public

Note: The mortgage should contain the following recital: "The execution of this mortgage has been duly authorized by the board of directors of the mortgagor."
See Section 911 of the Business Corporation Law.
Subdivision (e) of Section 715 of said law provides that the offices of president and secretary may not be held by the same person, except when that person owns all of the issued and outstanding stock of the corporation.

CERTIFICATE OF CORPORATE AGENT

Blumbergs Law Products T 379—Certificate by Corporate Agent as to Change of Address: BCL §805-A(b): 5-78.

Certificate of Change of

under Section 805-A of the Business Corporation Law

IT IS HEREBY CERTIFIED THAT:

(a) The name of the corporation is

and the corporation was formed under the (said) name

(b) The certificate of incorporation was filed by the department of state on the day of 19 .

(c) The certificate of incorporation is amended:

** to change the post office address to which the secretary of state shall mail a copy of any process against the corporation served upon him to*

** to change the address of the registered agent of the corporation to*

(d) A notice of the above proposed change of address was mailed to the corporation herein by the party signing this certificate, not less than thirty days prior to the date of the delivery hereof to the department of state and the corporation has not objected thereto; the party signing this certificate is:

** the agent of the corporation to whose address the Secretary of State is required to mail copies of process.*

** the registered agent.*

* Strike out if inapplicable.

IN WITNESS WHEREOF, *this certificate has been subscribed this day of 19 by the undersigned who affirm(s) that the statements made herein are true under the penalties of perjury.*

Type name	*Capacity in which signed*	*Signature*
....	....	....
....	....	....
....	....	....

 333—Certificate of Dissolution, Business Corporation Law.

Certificate of Dissolution of

under Section 1003 of the Business Corporation Law

IT IS HEREBY CERTIFIED THAT:

(1) The name of the corporation is

(2) The certificate of incorporation was filed by the department of state on the day of 19

(3) The name, title and address of each of its officers and directors are:

Name	Title	Street and Number

(4) The corporation elects to dissolve.

*(5) * The dissolution was authorized at a meeting of shareholders by vote of the holders of two-thirds of all the outstanding shares entitled to vote.*
** The dissolution was authorized by unanimous written consent of the holders of all the outstanding shares entitled to vote thereon.*
** The dissolution was authorized pursuant to and in the manner required by the provisions of the certificate of incorporation authorizing dissolution, which provisions are as follows:*

* strike out if inapplicable

IN WITNESS WHEREOF, ***this certificate has been subscribed on 19 by the undersigned who affirm(s) that the statements made herein are true under the penalties of perjury.***

Type name	(Registered) Agent	Signature
....	....	....

RESERVATION OF CORPORATE NAME

T 284—Application for Reservation of Corporate Name. BCL & N-PCL, 10-82.

Department of State
Division of Corporations
Albany, New York 12231

Sirs:

Application is hereby made to reserve a corporate name and the following is set forth in support of the application. This application is made pursuant to the ☐ Business Corporation Law.
☐ Not-for-Profit Corporation Law.

(1) Applicant's name and address –

(2) Name to be reserved –

(3) The basis for the reservation is –

☐ Applicant intends to form a domestic corporation.

☐ Applicant, a domestic corporation, intends to change its name.

☐ Applicant a foreign corporation, intends to make application for authority to do business in this state.

☐ Applicant, an authorized foreign corporation, intends to change its name.

☐ Applicant intends to incorporate a foreign corporation under the laws of the state of
and have said foreign corporation apply for authority to do business in this state.

☐ Applicant is a foreign corporation. It intends to use a fictitious name because its name (in its original jurisdiction) is not available in New York State.

(4) The nature of the business to be conducted.

(5) The location of the principal office will be in the county of

(6) Accompanying this application is a certified check for $20.

Very truly yours,

....
Type name of applicant

by..
Signature

Certificate of reservation to be sent to:

☐ Applicant at above address

☐ Agent..

address..

....

☐ Attorney..

address..

....

APPENDIX III

HELPFUL IRS PUBLICATIONS

The Internal Revenue Service makes available a number of publications covering specific areas of tax law. These publications can be quite helpful for both the shareholders of the corporation and the officers and directors running the business. Publication numbers and areas of coverage are:

1: Your Rights as a Taxpayer
15: Circular E—Employer's Tax Guide
334: Tax Guide for Small Business
393: Federal Employment Tax Forms
463: Travel, Entertainment, and Gift Expenses
505: Tax Withholding and Estimated Tax
509: Tax Calendars
510: Excise Taxes
533: Self-Employment Tax
534: Depreciation
535: Business Expenses
536: Net Operating Losses
537: Installment Sales
538: Accounting Periods and Methods
539: Employment Taxes
542: Tax Information on Corporations
544: Sales and Other Dispositions of Assets
545: Interest Expense
548: Deductions for Bad Debts
549: Condemnations and Business Casualties and Thefts
550: Investment Income and Expenses
551: Basis of Assets
556: Examination of Returns, Appeal Rights, and Claims for Refund
560: Retirement Plans for the Self-Employed

583: Taxpayers Starting a Business
587: Business Use of Your Home
589: Tax Information on S Corporations
590: Individual Retirement Arrangements (IRAs)
910: Guide to Free Tax Services
911: Tax Information for Direct Sellers
916: Information Returns
917: Business Use of a Car
925: Passive Activity and At-Risk Rules
937: Business Reporting

WHERE TO GET IRS PUBLICATIONS AND FORMS

The preceding IRS publications listed can be obtained from the IRS Forms Distribution Center serving your location.

If you are located in Alaska, Arizona, California, Colorado, Hawaii, Idaho, Montana, Nevada, New Mexico, Oregon, Utah, Washington, or Wyoming, write to Rancho Cordova, CA 95743-0001.

If you are located in Alabama, Arkansas, Illinois, Indiana, Iowa, Kansas, Kentucky, Louisiana, Michigan, Minnesota, Mississippi, Missouri, Nebraska, North Dakota, Ohio, Oklahoma, South Dakota, Tennessee, Texas, or Wisconsin, write to P.O. Box 9903, Bloomington, IL 61799.

If you are located in Connecticut, Delaware, District of Columbia, Florida, Georgia, Maine, Maryland, Massachusetts, New Hampshire, New Jersey, New York, North Carolina, Pennsylvania, Rhode Island, South Carolina, Vermont, Virginia, or West Virginia, write to P.O. Box 25866, Richmond, VA 23289.

If you are located in Puerto Rico, write to Richmond, VA. If you are located in the Virgin Islands, write to the V.I. Bureau of Internal Revenue, Lockharts Garden No. 1A Charlotte Amalie, St. Thomas, VI 00802.

INDEX